I0421915

HOW TO ANALYZE PEOPLE

A complete guide for everyone; Body languages,
manipulation and dark psychology

DISCLAIMER

The information contained within this eBook is strictly for educational purposes. If you wish to apply ideas contained in this eBook, you are taking full responsibility for your actions.

The author has made every effort to ensure the accuracy of the information within this book was correct at time of publication. The author does not assume and hereby disclaims any liability to any party for any loss, damage, or disruption caused by errors or omissions, whether such errors or omissions result from accident, negligence, or any other cause.

WHY YOU SHOULD READ THIS BOOK

To be successful in politics, leadership, or any of a number of things including sales, negotiation, diplomacy, and business it would behoove you to find a way to get these same skills and talents for yourself. If you'd like to find a way to better your career in this regard, This book is a decent book which pits body types against personalities and preferences of those you meet.

This book isn't the only method people use for figuring out others, but it seems to be easier and more efficient than asking someone their Zodiac sign and then telling them to hold that thought while you go figure out exactly what that means. This book talks about psychology, body language, body type, and is an overall human analysis that will help you judge those you meet and be spot on a good percentage of the time. In fact, as you read this book, you'll start to see how accurate it is based on those friends, associations, family members and people you already know.

Apparently, things have changed a lot over the years in our society and civilization, but not so much has changed in human behavior. So, you'd be wise to get a quick education on all this and then use this knowledge to develop your own skills along this line when you try to figure out those personalities and human types you meet. Is this really profiling? You bet it is, and it seems to work.

TABLE OF CONTENTS

INTRODUCTION

Why should you smile? Smiling is one of the special aspects of a human being. It is the best way to show your great mood as well as to share the happy feelings to others. Smiling is also a symbol to express your love, friendship, and care that will be recognized by others as something that comes from your heart. In addition, a gesture shows your self-confidence.

Some people say that smiling is transmittable or contagious because no one wants to live in cranky community or world; they prefer to spare their time to those people who always wear a smile on their face and have a great laugh. In this article, you will be able to find out why you should smile and why it is important in our lives.

Why people should smile? There are several reasons why people need to smile. There is a saying that smiling makes you live longer because it is the way to be more positive in any aspect of life that will lead us to a healthier and a happier living. We can attain more health benefits in smiling, too. Most of the doctors said laughter is the best medicine.

Smile reduces stress and makes you relaxed. So have a smile to improve your lifespan and that is a priceless gift that you can give to everyone. Giving the sweetest smile to someone will ease his or her problems and lone-liness. Most of the songs make us smile and it is the best therapy for depressions.

Another health benefit of smiling is strengthening of our immune system. An emerging healing effect shows how smile can be a best therapy for faster healing among any other thing. When you smile it strengthen more muscles on your face and it prevents to look like old. There are ten best reasons why you should smile always, and these are:

1. It administers your hormones.

2. Smile lessens the level of the stress hormones. It is like a cortisol, adrenaline, epinephrine, growth hormone, and dopamine. It also helps to boost the level of the health-enhancing hormones such as neurotransmitters, and endorphins as well as the antibody-producing cells and effectively enhance of the T cells. Those are the benefits-to have a strong immune system.

3. Good internal workout.

4. A good smile and a belly laugh can be an exercise for the face and the diaphragm. It makes us look younger because of the thou-sands of muscles that undergo a workout when we are smiling as well as when we laugh. This

workout will leave the muscles and shoulders stronger. Lastly, it gives a great workout for our heart.

5. Physically Free.

6. Did you come to a time that you want to smile or cry? Moreover, did you experience the feeling after you had a good laugh and great smile? Well, laughter and smile provides the best emotional and physical release.

7. A positive outlook of mind.

8. Smile brings your center of attention away from guilt, anger, negative emotions, and stress. It will boost your self-confidence and makes you happy.

9. Change your point of view.

10. Some studies say the best response for the stressful events is a smile or laughter. Smile can give you more light in your points of view and it will help us to view the all the challenges and threats positively and conquer them by having a positive point of view.

11. Social Benefits of Smile.

12. A smile always connects us to others. As I mentioned above, it is contagious, if you smile,

the world will smile back at you. You can help those people to smile more and realize the benefits of it. You can elevate the mood of those people around you by giving them the best smile and you can also improve the value of the social interaction with different kinds of people. The more you show your smile with them, the more they will smile too. Smile helps us to reminisce those happy moments more vibrantly. We feel more positive and optimistic as well as motivated.

13. 7. Smile will fight against illness.

14. Optimistic people have a high immune systems and that is the best way to beat any illness. According to the study of optimism, there is a connection between the good health and the optimistic attitudes. Most of the optimistic persons are healthier and they have more vigorous immune system.

15. 8. Longer Lifespan.

16. According to the study of psychiatry, most elderly at the age of 65 up to 85 are optimistic. They believe that it is better to expect good things rather than to expect bad ones.

17. 9. It makes you feel like you eat two thousand chocolate bars.

18. A smile gives same level of eating chocolate. Why? The researchers determined heart and brain activities have the same depiction of smiling if they receive money and some bars of chocolates.

10. Smile will absolutely cost nothing.

19. Smile is the ambassador of your good will. It brightens up the life of those people who see someone smiling on them. It is like a sunrise that gives light to dark clouds.

Therefore, it is very important to a person to learn how to smile and why we should smile.

CHAPTER 1
HOW TO SPOT A FAKE SMILE
FROM A GENUINE ONE

Have you ever been so angry at someone that you smiled at them? It's actually quite scary when the person realizes how furious you are. Like a hat, there is a different smile for almost every occasion. Excited, joyful, exhausted, angry, morose, contented, wry, crooked, half-smile and more are all different smiles that can be used to convey an exact emotion. These different smiles are often more telling about a person's state of being when put in context.

For example, when your husband arrives home late, after the children are tucked in, holding his worn briefcase after a four day business meeting; he ambles slowly across the room to sit down beside you and starts to remove his shoes. As he looks at you his eyes look sad, but he is smiling a crooked, tired smile. He is saying, "Don't worry, everything will be okay. I love you."

Happy, Contented, Joyful

These are what you think of when you think of someone smiling, a pleasant smile, a comforting smile. This is a smile that emanates a glow of warmth to those around. These smiles can have different reactions to those around. If someone is already in a bad mood, these smiles can further irritate, but if someone else is happy too, these smiles can further augment how contented or happy one feels.

Sarcastic, Wry, Spiteful

Who would have thought that a smile could be so negative, but the truth is that a smile can be, at times, one of the best ways to convey these types of emotions. Physically this smile is very, very small; almost unnoticeable. However, the implications are very deep, as if this person knows something you don't, or he wants to cause you harm. This smile is almost never present on its own, and typically comes with an entire facial expression and posture to grab your attention, but when you look under all of that the smile is revealed in it's true, malicious form.

Excited, Ecstatic

This is a hard smile to actually see, because for the most part the person wearing is jumping around the room. However, once you get them to finally sit still the smile is revealed to all the public. It is a bright and happy smile, but it is nearly uncontainable. The smile seems to emanate from the lips with such ferocity that it seems to threaten to break out of the edges of the face, itself.

Crooked, Solemn, Morose

This is the smile described at the beginning. This is the strong, but sad smile of the loving guardian bearing the weight of the world so that those he loves aren't crushed by it. It usually accompanies very sad, but strong eyes in those it resides in. You can find this smile in more than just suburban patriarchs if you look hard enough. When you open your eyes to what's around you, you can find this smile in anyone who has something worth fighting for.

Half-smile, Confident

Physically, this can look like the crooked smile, but the half-smile is found in an entirely different context. This smile is worn on the face of someone completely confident and self-assured, but only for a brief moment. It could also be considered a smile of serious amusement. It shows up upon receiving a compliment occasionally, or when someone, intent on their work, finds something humorous for a brief instance.

Cute, Coy

While these are definitely NOT the same, the physical aspects of it are very similar, and they both try to cause the person seeing the smile to imply something about the person smiling. A cute smile portrays a sense of innocence, while a coy smile tries to portray possible future events. The coy smile is one of the most manipulative smiles in the entire arsenal.

Do you know that by knowing and applying the body language secrets in the chapters of this book, you can easily boost up your social and working life tremendously. You will also develop all the skills to have complete power and full control in any situation, thus giving you a very big edge over others.

It's now time for you to open up to success, let your body speak up for you, and change your life for the better.

CHAPTER 2
LEARN HOW TO INTERPRET THE TOP THREE TYPES OF BODY LANGUAGE SMILE

Did you know that a smile can be used to convey many and different kinds of inner feelings. From big and broad smiles to enchanting smiles, from polite courteous smiles to fake smiles, from shy smiles to lopsided uneven smiles. Many nuances of emotion can actually be displayed by this simple gesture.

A recent research has identified the three main kinds of smile, each on its own connoting a different type of emotion. With a little practice, it is possible to distinguish between the Heartfelt Smile, the Gloomy Smile and the Counterfeit Smile as they all need different use of facial muscles to be performed.

1. The Heartfelt Smile

This is known as the straight from the heart, genuine and sincere smile. The true and impulsive feelings of pure joy, gladness, happiness, amusement and pleasure are spontaneously expressed through this smile.

The facial muscles will raise the corners of the mouth, while both the cheeks will be lifted up and at the same time retracting the skin around the eye socket inwards. The stronger the emotion gets, the more distinct this muscle action will become. This heartfelt smile normally only last between two-thirds of a second to four seconds and it is very seldom held longer than that.

Basically this kind of smile is divided into three categories that consist of the simple smile, the upper smile and the broad smile. The simple smile will appear when the mouth turns up while the lips remained closed. It denotes a personal private pleasure and it is most often seen when people are smiling to themselves.

The upper teeth are usually exposed during the upper smile. Combined with a simultaneous eye contact, this is the most common smile used by people when greeting one another. As for the broad smile, both the upper and lower sets of teeth will be exposed, this smile will normally grow broader and broader until it becomes a laugh. Eye contact is very minimal during this type of smile.

2. The Gloomy Smile

This type of smile can be easily defined by its asymmetrical, lopsided and wry shape. Half the mouth will look like smiling while the other half frowning at the same time. This smile is usually displayed in front of others by someone who is conceding failure, defeat or unhappiness.

3. The Counterfeit Smile

A counterfeit smile is also more asymmetrical compared to a sincere and genuine smile, and it is an intentional gesture performed to mislead and deceive others. This kind of fake smile usually last longer than a heartfelt smile, and more time is needed for it to spread across the face.

Many examples of the counterfeit smile can be seen from the faces of inexperienced actors, shady politicians, dishonest salesmen and all those other people whose job requires smiling all the time.

So how do you actually distinguish and differentiate a counterfeit smile from a genuine straight from the heart smile? The most noticeable giveaway is from the eyes, which will squint, crinkle up and becomes narrower when the smile actually comes from the heart genuinely. On the contrary, the eyes will remain the same and unaffected when someone is smiling falsely to hide away negative emotions. Always start by observing the corner of the eyes for smile lines, and then check closely at the mouth area for a raised upper lip and a flat square lower lip.

Most people will be able to notice and sense the discordant expressions between a real heartfelt smile and a fake counterfeit smile. A fake smile will only be able to cover up the negative emotions for a short period of time, for it creates an uneasy and constrained feeling within the observer who may instinctively know that something is wrong and amiss. The fact is when someone is truly smiling from the heart, the facial muscles around the eyes cannot be brought under conscious control by the mind, thus making the mouth the only part which can lie.

CHAPTER 3
HOW TO KNOW WHAT PEOPLE WANT

Do you often ask yourself? What does my new client want, is he or she looking for my product or service? What does my wife or my husband want, sometimes I just don't understand? What does my boss want, sometimes I think I know just to find out I'm wrong? These and many similar questions linger in our minds and perplex us. We all know what we want or need at any given moment of the day but what is it that other people want?

All people are concerned first and foremost with their needs or problems, most of the time. They are the main character in their story. And while they may generally care for other people their thoughts are focused on themselves, even in caring for others it is in relation to them selves. So ask yourself, how can I know exactly what they want? Remember this; find their interests with probing questions, what is that they are passionate about. If you are visiting a new client's office have a look around while you are waiting and observe and make note of the surroundings. Are things neat and in order? What is the color scheme of the room? Is there artwork, trophies or family pictures?

Here are three rules to remember when dealing with people: listen, listen, and listen!

Have you ever met someone you didn't like right off the bat? Of course you have, we all have. Did that person seemed uncaring or cold to you and seemed to treat people as though he or she was better than everyone else? Then let that person be your challenge. The next time you meet someone like this engage them in conversation. Be genially happy to meet them. Say things like "Hi how are you? It's good to meet you." Comment on how nice there hair looks or how much you like what they are wearing. Only respond to their questions briefly and turn the conversation back them. Respond to them with a lot of "really I didn't know that" or "that's great". The point is let them talk no matter how much you want to talk about what you want or like. What it all comes down to is they will like you because they feel you like them. So give it a try you may just make a friend for life.

THE SMILE MYTH

A great smile is important to your success in life. You can't argue with that. And if you want to improve your customer service in business, a great strategy is to tell all your front line people to smile! Well, maybe not.

Here's the catch. Not all smiles are created

equal. Genuine smiles and fake smiles don't have the same power and impact. And secondly, genuine smiles are not produced by executive decree. To believe otherwise is to believe a myth.

Without even knowing it, our "fake" detector is always turned on. We unconsciously read body language, facial signals, giving us an impression whether a smile is genuine or plastic.

Have you ever met someone and felt that you had been thrown a fake smile? A salesman? Someone at a singles bar? Your in-laws? Actually, you could list almost any group as occasionally guilty of less-than-genuine smiles.

Having a customer warm up to a sales person or front-line greeter is more complicated than a genuine or fake smile. A good, trusting relationship doesn't happen at the snap of a finger or the flash or a smile. A solid relationship is complex and it takes time. Let's examine some of the considerations and factors that help us understand promoting good customer service, good first impressions, and good relationships.

First, you can't mandate smiles for you subordinates. I love the story about teaching pigs to sing. It turns out to be an impossible task. "It frustrates the farmer and irritates the pigs." And I'll bet you that the farmer can't sing any better than the pigs in the first place.

You can't create smiles by demanding them. If that were possible, you'd be drowning in a sea of fake smiles. If you think that ordering smiles for your subordinates is a good strategy...go buy a case of wax lips.

Other factors leading to misguided smile strategies are: Sometimes our behavior gets in our way, and sometimes our thinking trips us up.

A common fallacy of human behavior is to dislike in others what we dislike about ourselves. A sarcastic person likely has little tolerance for other sarcastic people. A pushy person probably does not like to be pushed around by others. A person who never smiles is likely to be bugged by people who don't smile! Hence we have the grim-faced casino manager who wants to be surrounded by shimmering, smiling faces. As the street-wise would say, "Ain't gonna happen!"

On the flip-side, another fallacy of human behavior is to think that everyone is just like us. Or, closer to the truth, that everyone SHOULD be like us. If we have a great natural smile we feel like others should also beam a celebrity smile. But people are NOT like us. Due to culture, family upbringing, peer groups, genetics, medications, emotional states, bad teeth, and more...people are inclined or not inclined to smile. They are who they are. It's just the way it is.

Another fallacy is "what you see is what you get!" Not necessarily so. Interpreting human nature is more complex than just observing someone's smile. Just because a person isn't smiling doesn't mean he's unhappy. It doesn't mean she hates her job. It doesn't mean he dislikes working with customers. It doesn't mean that customers don't like her. Although a smiling worker is a terrific asset, there is a good chance that the more serious-looking worker connects better with the customer than the worker with the mandatory, plastic smile. Excellence at work is more complicated than the issue of To-Smile-or-Not-To-Smile.

And sometimes "what you see isn't what you get" because our reading of smiles is an art and not a science. When we see a smile, many times the impression of whether it's real or fake is correct, but sometimes it's wrong.

CHAPTER 4
WHY IT'S IMPORTANT TO CARE FOR YOUR SMILE

We all want that perfect, bright, straight smile that adorns the faces of the rich and famous. Some of us go to great lengths such as undergoing multiple cosmetic dental procedures to get the best smile possible.

Why are great-looking smiles important? The first thing most people think of is how their smile affects their appearance. We are attracted to people with beautiful smiles and we want to be one of those people.

With their intrinsic beauty aside, a bright, straight smile also offers many additional benefits.

Besides helping you look your best, here are some benefits a great smile can offer:

A beautiful smile is a healthy smile and vice versa. You can't expect to have an attractive smile if you don't properly care for it and it's unhealthy. When your smile is looking and feeling great, you win. A healthy mouth reduces your risk of tooth decay, gum disease, bad breath, missing teeth and oral cancer. Preventative dentistry is less expensive than restorative dentistry.

Your beautiful smile improves your relationships.

Want to be well liked? Want to be the person everyone wants to hang out with? I'm sure you do. Have you noticed a common characteristic of those people you enjoy being around? You've likely observed that they all laugh and smile. You won't smile often if you have a smile that can use some improvement and which you think is mediocre at best.

A beautiful smile can open up job opportunities. Did you know that smiling not only makes you irresistible to friends, but also to employers and other business professionals? Why? Because people in business see individuals who smile as being more sure and confident. Successful leaders are those who have charisma, which entails smiling and showing off those pearly whites.

Your beautiful smile can make you happier. Those who laugh and smile frequently experience more happiness, peacefulness and contentment. They also experience less stress. The chemicals released from smiling and laughing have been shown to improve your mood as well as the mood of those around you.

A beautiful smile means a healthier you. Studies have linked the health of one's mouth to one's overall health. Heart disease and high blood pressure can be a side effect of not smiling, which can be caused by an unhealthy mouth. Diabetes can increase one's risk of cavities. Infections of the teeth, such as teeth abscess can cause potentially severe, deadly blood infections. The happy thoughts and positive thinking that comes from smiling can also boost one's immune system, allowing it to better fight disease.

A beautiful smile can lengthen your life. The culmination of a healthy social life, self-confidence, and happy thoughts can help you live longer.

A beautiful smile is more than skin deep. Besides enhancing your appearance, a smile can offer multiple health benefits. Because your smile is important, great care is needed. Both, proper at-home oral hygiene and regular dental office visits are necessary to maintain and improve your smile. If it has been longer than six months, it is recommended that you schedule an appointment with your dentist. A bright, straight, beautiful smile is possible with great, regular dental care.

CHAPTER 5
BETRAYED BY BODY
LANGUAGE

If you have read anything about body language, the chances are you have heard that 90% of communication is non-verbal. The actual origin of this slightly distorted statistic is the research of Dr. Albert Mehrabian who concluded in his 1971 study Silent Messages that communication in every conversation is 7% words, 38% sound of voice and 55% facial expression. Consequently, the 90% (or rather 93%) of all communication is body language is born. However, it would be wrong to assume that the majority of communication is made through body language. In everyday life, we don't usually negate what people say, so what becomes interesting about body language and how body language become useful is in relation to what is being said.

For patients with advanced dementia, phsyical appearance is a significant factor in the assessment of pain because of the reduced ability for verbal communication, but in almost other cases a nurse would not rely on how a patient is acting to suggest how much pain a patient is in, they would ask the patient. Similarly, if someone is sitting with their arms and legs crossed and has an annoyed look on their face, you are probably not going to talk to them. In this case, body language is 100% of the communication, but the only way to make sure is to speak to them. Body language betrays you by exposing your feelings and attitude, yet it is your words and their relation to your body language that are truly central to your communication.

Despite the importance of body language in communication, without the verbal part of the communication, non-verbal communication is quite limited. It is the combination of words and body language that betrays you, especially when what you say and how you act do not match. Mehrabian labelled congruence or consistency between body language and words to be a crucial element of the study of non-verbal communication; looking for when a person's words and actions do or do not match.

But surely if a person hasn't studied body language you have nothing to worry about? Before there were books on body language, people were picking up on the signs without being total aware of what they were picking up on. When someone says they are happy but don't act happy, you aren't going to need a book on body language to help you read the signs. Even if the person you have been talking has not read the books, it is highly likely that your body language will betray you.

As you venture out into your day to day dealings with

other people, what you need to be concerned with is not how you act, but how you act in relation to what you say. Your body language can be all erratic and excited if you are saying excited things, but, if you act erratic when you are lying, the situation is different.

But, if you are telling the truth, why would you want to fake body language? The answer is simply that we are only human. When we say nice things to our partners or talk to our bosses, sometimes we are just too tired or just not interested. We can be talking about the one thing that we think is the most interesting or exciting thing in the world, but if we are hungry, or tired, or ill, or just having a bad day, the words we use might be enthusiastic but our body language will betray us.

How do you fake it? Most experts say you can't fake body language. This is good news if you have read 'top ten signs she likes you' or 'how to tell if he is lying.' But if you are trying to make yourself look good then, this could be a problem.

So what do we do? The simple answer is we increase the incongruence between what we say and our body language. We increase incongruence in two ways:

This first thing we can do is be honest. Don't try to sound too enthusiastic if you are not. If you are feeling tired don't try and compensate by being overly excited. You can be excited, but don't over do it. If you disagree with someone don't lie to them. As much as possible, merely avoid directly answering them. So, when your girlfriend or friend asks "Do I look fat in this?" respond with a "You look great" or "You look good in that dress" and then try to change the subject. Whether you say yes or no, you are probably lying. So don't answer the question. Don't avoid the subject, but don't directly answer the question.

The second thing we can do is to be aware of how you are acting and do something different. Congruence is about continuity, if you cast doubt on the continuity of the signs, you should be able to make reading them difficult and so disrupt congruence.

Although telling the truth can be a delicate business, disrupting the congruence of your body language will require you to think about how you are feeling and to know a little something about body language. It doesn't require a great deal of information, but you should be aware that body language is usually considered to function in clusters, so what you are doing with your arms is only relevant if it relates to the expression on your face and how you are standing. When you need to ensure someone is not reading everything about you from your body language, you will want to break down the clusters of your actions and consequently disrupt congruence.

Areas of body language to focus on:

Facial expressions: if you are feeling bored then show interest, if you are happy show a little sadness, if you have nothing to say make like you want to say something. When whoever you are speaking to gives you the opportunity to speak and you don't, they will begin to question their own understanding of you.

Eye contact: the failure to maintain eye contact shows lack of interest or deception. Aggressively maintained eye contact displays a desire to dominate another person. Judge your own feelings and intentions and adjust eye contact accordingly.

Touch: attraction is displayed by physical touch. In a dating situation, if a woman begins to touch, however innocently, another person, she is showing interest in them. Avoid inappropriate touching. In the workplace, inappropriate touching is anything more than a handshake. Do touch in interpersonal relationships. You might feel tried, but your partner will really appreciate that hug.

Arms and legs: your posture betrays all kinds of things about you. Two elements to be aware of are pointing arms and legs and the open or closed body posture. Often we show interest in someone by pointing our arms and legs towards them. If we are not interested and ready to go, we may point our limbs towards the door in an effort to be ready when it really is time to go. On a very basic level the open or closed body posture is the difference between crossed arms and legs and uncrossed arms and legs. The closed body says "I am not interested or listening." An open body says the opposite.

Tone of voice: how do you speak normally? Are you a loud fast talker, a slow quite speaker? Think about how you sound when you are angry. Don't get too carried away. You don't want the boss to think you are aggressive when you are just tired, but do think about volume, speed, tone and infusing your voice with a little emotion.

Your body language is going to betray you. An uncontrollable incongruence between how you are acting and what you are saying is going say something you don't want it to. Think about what you want to say and how you feel, and then do something else entirely. A little disruption goes a long way.

Disrupting body language can be hard work and is not something you would want to do all the time. If you use it regularly on an unusually perceptive friend, they will pick up on your signals and see through your strategy. If you disrupt congruence when you are feeling uncertain, you can fight back against the betrayal of body language.

CHAPTER 6
A WIDE, BRIGHT SMILE

In a world full of reasons to brood and be upset about, there is only one thing that can bring in some hope. A wide, bright SMILE.

Mother Teresa once said, "Every time you smile at someone, it is an action of love, a gift to that person, a beautiful thing!" It is so true. Even when you are having a bad day or things aren't going the way you want them to, a simple smile, even from someone whom you may not know, can actually make your day better. Especially when it comes from little children! Probably because children have the most honest and innocent smiles. They strike a chord immediately.

Such a simple thing and yet it has an effect that can turn your entire day around. And yet we are such sticklers when it comes to showing our teeth (literally)! It almost seems like we don't smile because it requires effort! So, today I am going to list down some of the best reasons for you to smile!

Here you go:

1. Smiling requires less effort than frowning!

Not kidding! You probably learned in school. But just

in case, let me refresh your memory. It takes fewer muscles to smile, than it does to frown. Many scientific theories have lately discounted this fact, but the truth is, why believe them?!

As far as I am concerned, smiling requires less effort, since you don't have any mental stress or worry when you smile. Whereas if you are frowning, you obviously are discontent with something!

2. Makes you look good

If you've paid attention, you must have noticed. Even someone who doesn't have the whole Greek God look, can end up looking pretty fine with a smile! When you smile your face automatically brightens up. Your demeanour changes and you start spreading this happy vibe around you.

A study showed, that people with smiling faces are 80% more likely to have a positive impact, on the people around them. So be it a business meeting or a date, a gorgeous smile is your secret weapon to success!

So irrespective of what you don't wear, Do wear a Smile.

3. Smiling is contagious!

When you smile, you automatically trigger a connection with the person you are smiling at. That person, whoever they maybe, is then almost psychologically forced to smile. And just like a domino effect, smiles keep passing on. So that's one contagious thing that you can happily spread everywhere!

4. Good first impression

Interview tip 101. Always greet people with a smile. Even if you meet them for the first and the last time. A smile is absolutely essential. When you smile on entering a room or meeting someone, you have a great first impression. You spread this positive aura and people feel this natural affinity to you. They may even take special note of your pleasant approach and remember you in future exchanges.

This helps a lot, especially if the person in front is someone who is influential and can be of some help to you in the future. They will remember you by face, even if they forget your name! And even if that person is nobody important to you, it's always nice to have a familiar face around when you are in a crowd.

5. Fights Wrinkles!!!

If you've ever wanted to grow old with as few wrinkles as possible, SMILE! When you smile, the creases on your forehead automatically even out and you have lesser chance of having fine lines and wrinkles as you age.

Conversely, when you frown too much, your forehead creases too often and the number of lines on your forehead and around your lips increase.

So avoid the frown and adopt the smile!

What more could you want?? Free treatment for wrinkles! So kick the anti-aging creams and smile it out. Now that you know about all the benefits, you can find the motivation to go ahead and try smiling more.

To add to this, if you need reasons to keep smiling, here are a few:

✓ You're alive and well

✓ You have beautiful people who love you so much!

✓ Life is full of unexplored opportunities and you get to go on an adventure every single day.

✓ Yesterday is over, but there is a brighter tomorrow waiting to be embraced.

✓ You have a face. You have a responsibility to make it look amazing. So, Smile!

✓ Smile because you can. Because you feel like it and that's one thing you can do free of cost!

CHAPTER 7
BODY LANGUAGE IN SPORTS

Aristotle said that man is a "social animal" and a "linguistic animal." This convention is so anchored in our perception that it is hard to believe when psychologists claim that 90% of our communication is not verbal at all.

The meaning of this fact is simple - we communicate and transmit many messages, without uttering a word. Chazal (the old Talmudic sages) said that life and death are in the hands of the tongue, but as soon as we realize that 90% of our communication is nonverbal, we must also be aware of the messages we convey in our nonverbal communication and how they affect those around us.

How do athletes get better?

Players learn to pass, kick, shoot, attack, stop, change direction, close running lines and many other skills. As they improve these skills, they become better and more effective in the game. They improve these skills for two reasons:

Nonverbal communication in sports

If the psychologists are not mistaken and 90% of our communication is indeed nonverbal, why not apply the method of sports improvement even in relation to nonverbal communication? After all, this is a critical skill for the team's strength, which also affects the field during the game, during timeouts or breaks, in the dressing room and in training. The use of nonverbal communication in the group takes place at each meeting of the team players and throughout the encounter. The responsibility of the players and coaches is also, and perhaps first and foremost, to be aware of themselves and learn to communicate in a positive way.

Negative body language and team composition

I believe (mainly in children and youth departments) that a team must let go of a player, no matter how good he is, if he constantly "poisons" the group atmosphere with a negative body language. I also believe that a coach, no matter how good he is, whose body language regularly expresses negative messages to his players, shouldn't coach children and teens.

Universal body language

Studies indicate that body language is a universal language that crosses cultures, genders or physical limitations. When a blind-born athlete wins a competition, for example, he raises his hands in the air and looks up - although he has never seen anyone else express the sense of joy in winning this way. When that blind athlete loses, he pulls himself together, drops his shoulders and puts his hands on his face in a gesture of pain. Try to remember how soccer fans respond to the loss of their team - that's right, everyone responds the same way and "grabs the head" with both hands.

The myth of positive body language

There is a false myth, claiming that only players with a positive body language walk upright, open their shoulders, look straight and express their feelings with sharp, vigorous movements. This body language, claims the myth, expresses a winning attitude and can be seen looking at well-known winners such as Michael Jordan, Zlatan Ibrahimovic and Cristiano Ronaldo. These players are a model indeed. But not for everyone.

Body Language Models

Every person is motivated by different motivations and the difference between people must be respected. Therefore, one must also accept a different body language: less external, but present. This body language expresses peace of mind and focus on action, and is clearly represented by players such as Messi, Iniesta, Nowitzki and Tim Duncan. Does anyone suspects that Messi or Tim Duncan are not Winners? Their teammates have come to know how they express positivity or winning attitude, and so does the audience. There is a wide variety of legitimate positive nonverbal body language expressions, and each player can find what is right for him. What he can't do any more in modern sports is being unaware of his nonverbal communication, or being aware of his negative nonverbal communication - and sticking to it nonetheless.

Active communication = cohesion

Try once to do the following experiment: Watch a basketball game without sound and pay particular attention to the nonverbal communication of the players. In no time you will notice how the players communicate using physical gestures without words: often you will see a player raise his eyebrows to indicate to his friend that he is ready for a move. A point guard will turn his chest toward the player he wants to give the ball to, half a second before the actual delivery - and thus send him a message to be ready. The chin and eyes also become effective communication tools when the hands hold the ball. Pay attention how the shooting players lifts his thumb in the air to mark his appreciation after a good assist, or the pats on the buttocks. All these examples demonstrate the effectiveness and power of positive nonverbal communication. This kind of communication attests to an understanding between the players and high group cohesion. This good communication can also help an inferior team beat a better team.

The body language of each individual is derived from his or her level of self-awareness, personality, and mental abilities. If you know how hard it is to change physical habits in the game, such as keeping a low body, maintaining stability during delivery, and scanning the area before getting the ball, you will understand how difficult it is to change embodied sub-conscious patterns - body language patterns that we have become accustomed to.

How do you change a negative body language?

When a coach or a player feels that their body language is negative, they must change it. This change will not only improve the atmosphere in training and games but also make the team better. Anyone who can receive support from a psychologist who specializes in communications should do so.

If you are a coach and cannot assign players such an escort, you can still drive a change process based on the following points:

1. Psychological understanding - Understanding the effect of particular skill on their play creates the motivation to work hard and improve

2. Physical practice - they work hard and thus improve

    A. Present the importance of team communication at the first training sessions

    B. Learn and diagnose, during the first trainings, the body language of each player in your team

3. When you summarize the training sessions, also refer to the energy level. Set a score scale for the level of energy that trainings should be conducted in. When the team fails to achieve that index, react decisively.

4. Find videos of players with a negative body language and players with a positive body language. Show them to your players and analyze the feelings and messages they receive. In the first stage, analyses of a third person are more effective. Find varied examples and try to avoid the classic and familiar, e.g. Michael Jordan and Cristiano Ronaldo.

5. Develop a mutual language with your players. After they'll express identification with a player with a positive body language, remind them, during training sessions, how the player behaves or his name

6. film players who failed to make a change and edit the negative body language expressions to create a short clip. show them the clip in private, and discuss with them their feelings. Sometimes such a reflection would do the trick

7. Make it clear that they are allowed to feel "fake" at first. That the gap between what they feel and what they express is legitimate. However, what they

express is more important because it affects the team

8. If the player has not been able to get rid of his negative body language, refer him for professional help and take a clear position on this subject

CHAPTER 8
THE IMPACTS OF A SMILE MAKEOVER

The underlying yet spreadable influence of a beautiful smile is radiant health, happiness, and invitation. A "Smile Makeover," a commonly used term for many Americans today, is drafted to magnify the exquisite and functional features of teeth through cosmetic and restorative dental procedures leaving one with a sparkling, whiter, more young looking smile. Our eyes and smile are the only context of face that speak to us. And when you smile they both light up.

A pretty smile is an image of ones inner state and overall health. Many people view this as an indication of how you take care of yourself. A new smile can have the following impacts:

Dopamine: When you smile, your brain automatically releases some chemicals that make your body feel that you are happy. Even if you are not happy inside but smiling, brain still releases dopamine that makes you feel better.

Confidence: Smile can easily attract people towards you. There is less effort done in smiling than frowning. A good smile provides more dimension and beauty to your face. It makes you visible.

Smiling is contagious: When you approach people with an amazing smile on your face, it can change the reactions of the people in front of you. When you smile, they will also smile. A smile is actually contagious. There are a lot of people who look different by getting new dentures. They look amazingly new and fresh with that beautiful smile.

Positivity: Your state of mind can be changed by an amazing smile. Even if you sad, lonely and unhappy, a smile can make you positive. Smile makeovers can transform your world in an amazing new world.

IT IS ALL IN THE SMILE

There are many interesting experiments conducted to study the impacts of cosmetic dental surgery on other's perceptions. Patients of cosmetic surgery looked more attractive after the surgery. They were more likely to enjoy success with the opposite sex and looked more wealthier.

When compared the "before" and "after" photos of the patients, the changes were really visible and subtle. The main difference was the fact that the changes in these photos could often be quite subtle, as some people had relatively little work done on their teeth. The main difference was the fact that they were more confident after the surgery and were able to shine with their smiles.

Even Small Changes Can Create a Big Difference

A smile makeover doesn't need to be striking but can have a far-reaching and positivity in your life. If you take a look at before and after photos of patients treated by cosmetic dentistry, then you will be able to see a huge difference. It is true that smile makeovers are not strictly imposed or a necessity because they are not a treatment for a disease. But the mental and psychological results are real big. People who had cosmetic dentistry. The state of mind can be changed by an amazing smile. Even if someone is sad, lonely and unhappy, a smile can make you positive. Smile makeovers can transform your world in an amazing new world.

CHAPTER 9
THE POWER OF A SINCERE
SMILE

Smiles show pleasure, happiness, amusement and humor. But smiles are also welcoming and friendly. Some smiles touch only the mouth but a sincere smile will reach the eyes.

When we smile we are more attractive and we stand out from those who are not smiling. It reduces our stress level and improves our health. Others are attracted and drawn to those who smile. Smiling elevates our moods, boosts our immune system, lowers our blood pressure, releases endorphins within our bodies, makes us look younger and helps us to stay positive. Smiling makes us more approachable and more optimistic. Smiles, like laughter, are contagious.

A smile can mean the world to a lonely person, to one with low self-esteem or little confidence and to someone who is feeling sad or depressed. A smile is powerful. It can make someone else feel happier and feel good about themselves. You can smile at strangers you meet on transit, while shopping, when you visit the doctor or dentist or anywhere else you go.

To encourage your own smiles, think about the things

that make you smile. Are they the antics of your children, the laughter of your grandchildren, a wink from your spouse, rocky road ice cream, sushi, dancing with someone special, the sun shining, a rainbow, crocuses poking their heads above the earth in early spring, a dog wagging its tail or a job well done?

The expression, fake it until you make it, could also apply to smiling. If you don't feel like smiling, smile anyway. But the more we smile, the more we feel that we genuinely want to smile. And the more we smile, the better we feel. The better we feel, the better those around us will feel. Therefore, it's easy to see that our smiles can create a domino effect.

Smiling also leads to thinking positively and a smile is a short hop away from laughter. Laughing is good for the heart, and like a smile is a pain and stress reliever. It is beneficial to the lungs, boosts immunity and because it is energizing, it can burn calories. Optimists smile more often than do pessimists. And optimists have better health. According to a recent study, a smile gives the same level of stimulation as eating 2,000 chocolate bars but is much better for the waistline. And when we smile, our voices sound warmer and more welcoming, making us more approachable.

A smile is recognized the world over and often no words are necessary when a person smiles in friendship.

When you go about your day, remember the power of a smile.

THINGS YOU OUGHT TO KNOW ON HOW TO SMILE WHEN YOU ARE SAD

Problems are inevitable in life because they are the ones that make us stronger and better persons. In trials, the lessons that we learned will keep us alive and wiser the next time to surpass others to come. They are just a piece of us as a whole and as life goes on.

The question is, how can you smile when you are sad? Is it possible for someone to smile even if he is sad? Probably, you might be thinking that they are just fake ones. Allow me to share with you the things you have to know on how to smile when you are sad. Most likely, they are tips and suggestions that you will need on how to smile when you are sad.

How to smile when you are sad, the common question ask by somebody who wants to forget something tragic or even just a little case of being upset. Strange it may seem but the smile is a hundred faces. Indeed, they are. You can smile differently depending on your mood and emotions. You will see the difference of every smile. First, let us talk about on how to smile when you are happy or on how to smile when you are funny. Laughter is far different from a smile. Why? They say that when you laugh, it has a sound and they are better than smile in terms of health because it can regulate the blood vessel to perform more actively by letting the good circulation of the blood. It happens that when you laugh, your heart pumps actively, resulting to release enough oxygen that will pass through the blood vessels and will make you feel better.

However, further studies that were conducted by some researchers found out that the smile when you are happy and the smile when you are funny has something to do with your good health too. As proven, they tested it many times in mixed ages of people and shows that the smile can send signal to the brain, and when your brain receives the message and detected that you are happy, some of your stress will be released.

Furthermore, you might be asking yourself a few questions about how to smile even if you feel that the world has turned its back on you. Among those questions include, how to smile when you are mad or how to smile when you are angry. Truly, this case will make it hard for us to show one true smile because we are on the act of getting mad about something or someone, depending on the purpose and on the severity of the reason. But still, you can take time to smile even if you are mad or angry.

Doctors advised that one should not take things seriously, meaning you do not have to be anxious about the world. If you keep this in your mind and let it be a part of your system, you can easily smile when you are mad. Try to remember that, perhaps, there is also an error on your part. Sometimes it is all in mind. And you just have work on it. Get out of the place and take a walk; it will help you to release adrenaline to make you feel better.

How you smile when you are depressed? How

to smile when you are sad? Here are some tips that you can use whenever you are sad and wanting to smile. Just think positively and sadness will go away.

1. Call a friend and try to detail the reason why you are sad.

2. Watch funny movies, particularly your favorite comedy movie.

3. Take a walk or anything that will make you sweat. They can make you release endorphins to make your body feel better, both emotional and physical.

4. Write or draw anything. You can release the bad energy through this.

5. Think of bad things happened in the past, and remember how well you did to surpass that situation.

6. Take a bath. You will be refreshed and will have a clear mind after.

7. Take a deep breath and breathe some fresh water outside. Do not trap yourself in depression.

8. Listen to the music and have a good cry. Allow your tears to fall down for a while and after that, switch the music into energetic tunes.

9. Take a nap.

These few things can help you on how to smile when you are sad. The bottom-line here, do not stress yourself and get trapped in depression. If you continue to do the old ways, you might end up with your days indulging with vices, such as drinking, smoking or the worse, taking up drugs. You can smile even if you are sad just try to remember and think of all the tips and suggestions I have given you on this article. Now you do not have to answer the question, how to smile when you are sad, you just have to act to move on with a smile on your face

SMILE AT EVERY NEW SITUATION

Many people fail to appreciate one of the simplest, most profound and best of all free gifts that human beings can bestow upon one another, and that is the smile. For many people the smile is an unconscious grace, something they offer to friends, acquaintances and passers-by alike without a second thought. For others, it is something that they consider difficult and struggle with. It is a source of endless awkwardness and agonizing; when is it appropriate to smile? Will they think I'm weird if I smile at them? Does my smile look all right? If this sounds like you, then it's important that you read the rest of this article in order to clear up a few things about smiling and why everybody should learn how to do it.

Your Smile is Fine

People today seem to attach way too much value to physical appearance in general. They're always worried how they look and what other people will think of them, and this may in part be because they themselves tend to make snap judgments based on looks. A smile, however, appeals to all people on a much deeper level, a more intuitive, natural level. While some people might form stereotypes based on the ways others dress or act, nobody is going around associating smiles with anything bad. Receiving a smile is universally considered a good thing, and invokes good feelings.

A Smile for Every Occasion

A good rule of thumb is that if you're not sure that it's appropriate to smile, smile anyway. Smiles are appropriate in almost every situation, and generally if they're not then you'll definitely know it. (In a hostage situation, the lack of smiling is not due to people wondering whether it's the right time to flash their captor's some teeth.) Smiling is becoming less and less common these days for precisely this reason, however: people get so hung up on the "right and wrongs" that they never get around to smiling. They're too nervous.

Forget about all of this and make it a habit to smile openly and genuinely every time you make eye contact with someone. You'll find that more people smile back than not, and gradually you'll derive more enjoyment from these simple exchanges. The whole experience actually becomes kind of a game.

Don't Take it Personally

So many people are nervous about smiling, don't take offense if you offer one to a stranger and don't get a smile in return. This is most likely because they were caught off guard or are self-conscious, not because they don't like you or don't like your smile. Remember the way you would act when people smiled at you, before you worked up the confidence to start smiling yourself.

Smiling is one of the easiest, simplest pleasures that humans can share with each other. They are natural, effortless (with a little practice) and infinitely rewarding. They have the potential to break the ice between strangers, form friendships between acquaintances and even brighten the lives of complete strangers more than you'll ever know. Take the time to practice at your smile, and to practice giving it freely to others, and you'll experience all these rewards and more firsthand.

SMILE - LOVE BEING YOU

It costs nothing, but creates much. It enriches those who receive, without impoverishing those who give. It happens in a flash and the memory of it sometimes lasts forever. How to win friends and influence people

Have you ever heard it takes more muscles to frown than it does to smile? It can take as little as five and as many as 16 to smile. Like any muscle the more you use your smile, the stronger it gets and the more smiling benefits you receive.

There are many health benefits to smiling, including increasing your sense of wellbeing and pleasure with each day. Smiling also improves your health by boosting your immune system and lowering your blood pressure. It's a great stress reliever and increases your attractiveness to others.

Smiling has been found to release powerful neurotransmitters like endorphins and serotonin - our body's natural 'feel good' drugs. Endorphins are also released when laughing, exercising, having sex, eating chocolate, sunbathing, during massages and meditation, when dancing, singing and listening to music - just about anything that leaves a smile on your face. Serotonin is a vital part of regulating our moods, sleep, sexuality and appetite. The serotonin/smile relationship goes both ways - good mood, getting good sleep, good sex and good food will ensure the smiles and serotonin keep coming.

The term "keep your chin up", has real physiological benefits. Notice what happens when you stretch your neck backward and look up - a natural smile forms in the facial muscles. There are many simple movements in the practice of yoga that produce this effect, which is probably why participants have a giant grin on their face after a yoga session.

While happiness comes at all ages, smiling into your golden years can actually promote longevity. In a study on optimism published in General Psychiatry, of those over the age of 65 optimists were 71 per cent less likely to die from certain causes than that of pessimists. A life full of smiles also exercises muscles in the face, which helps prevent drooping and saggy skin.

Here are some reasons smiling is good for us:

1. Smiling makes us attractive

We are drawn to people who smile. We want to know a smiling person and figure out what is making them smile. Frowns, scowls and grimaces all push people away, but a smile draws them in.

2.   Smiling changes our mood

Next time you are feeling down, try tricking your body by putting on a smile. There's a good chance you mood will change for the better.

3.   Smiling is contagious

When someone is smiling they light up the room, change the mood of others and make things happier. A smiling person brings happiness with them. Smile lots and you will draw people to you.

4.   Smiling relieves stress

Stress can really show up in our faces. Smiling helps to prevent us from looking tired, worn down and over-whelmed. When you are stressed, take time to put on a smile. The stress should be reduced and you will be better able to take action.

5.   Smiling boosts your immune system

When you smile immune function improves, possibly because you are more relaxed. Prevent the flu and colds by smiling.

6.   Smiling lowers your blood pressure

When you smile, there is a measurable reduction in your blood pressure. Sit for a few minutes and take your blood pressure. Then smile for a minute and take another reading while still smiling. Do you notice a difference?

7. Smiling releases natural feel good drugs

Studies have shown smiling releases endorphins, natural painkillers, and serotonin. Together these three make us feel good.

8. Smiling makes you look younger

The muscles we use to smile lift the face, making a person appear younger. Don't go for a facelift, just try smiling your way through the day - you'll look younger and feel better.

9. Smiling makes you seem successful

Smiling people appear more confident, are more likely to be promoted and to be approached. Put on a smile at meetings and appointments and people will react to you differently.

10. Smiling helps you stay positive

Try this test: smile. Now try to think of something negative without losing the smile. It's hard. When we smile our body is sending the message, "Life is good". Stay away from depression, stress and worry by smiling.

My favourite affirmation is, "I'm so happy I can't stop

smiling". It always helps put a smile on my face. If I don't feel like smiling, I try to "fake it until I make it". I pretend I am happy by smiling anyway and usually I find I am feeling better in no time.

Outrageously Healthy Tip: Practice smiling. When you are exercising, taking a walk or looking at yourself in the mirror tell yourself, "I'm so happy I can't stop smiling".

CHAPTER 10
IMPORTANCE OF SMILING
WHEN ATTRACTING WOMEN

"Life is like a mirror, we get the best results when we smile at it".

Of all the things you do when you approach a person, your smile is the most important. Happiness is often the motivating cause of a smile and if you approach a group while smiling, you will come across as relaxed, confident and fun. Also, most smiles are started by another smile as whatever you project to a person emotionally; they will generally project it back to you. Thus, if you can succeed in getting the group to smile and laugh in the first few seconds with you then you have successfully started the interaction and have made everybody in the group feel good.

The secret to how to attract women is to have a "giving" rather than a "taking" attitude. A smile costs nothing but gives much. It adds value to the group. It enriches those who receive and you use far less muscles than you do to frown. It takes a moment but is often the deciding factor on whether the group accept you or not. People are out in the bar to relax, have fun and enjoy themselves. Approaching the group without a smile is by far the biggest mistake that beginners make when they first begin working on this area of their lives. You only get one chance to make a first impression so use your smile. The more you make the group smile, the more easily you can build attraction with them. Everyone smiles in the same language and you never know who's falling in love with your smile.

By smiling, you will also have a positive effect on your own psychology. Many people feel that if you smile you are letting your guard down and it takes some of your power away. While smiling does show a little vulnerability, that makes it even more effective and powerful. The world always appears to be brighter when you smile. You will begin to think more positively and it will really help to put you in state. If you are having trouble smiling or you are simply not in a good mood, try laughing as this will easily transition into a smile. Picture something that made you laugh hysterically and that memory will help fuel a full blown smile. Have you ever heard the phrase

"Smile and the whole world smiles with you"

Not just any smile will do. You need to learn how to develop a genuine, infectious smile that can make people like you the moment they meet you and cause every group you approach to welcome you. Learn to develop your smile. You don't need perfect teeth to achieve a fantastic smile but they certainly do help. Keep your teeth clean. Regularly brushing your teeth and making sure your breath is fresh are some prerequisites to a good smile. If your teeth are less than white, get them cleaned or professionally polished.

Use your eyes to smile. People are only starting to finally realise that the eyes may actually be more essential to a warm, genuine smile than smiling with your mouth. To smile with your eyes, you slightly raise your cheekbones and lower your eyebrows, to give your eyes that twinkling effect. To become good at smiling with your eyes, practice smiling in front of a mirror, concentrating only on your eyes. Cover your mouth with your hand so you can only see your eyes. Practice smiling with your mouth only and your eyes only. Soon you will become aware of the muscles used to make your eyes smile and begin to use them every time you smile.

The secret is to approach while the smile is already on your lips and twinkling in your eyes before you make eye contact. It will seem natural when it is conveyed as how you are and not as something you do. If you open the group, make eye contact and then smile, you may come across as awkward and fake. The person will feel uncomfortable and you will not come across as a confident, fun guy but rather as somebody who has put her on the spot. If you approach and you already smiling or laughing, and you suddenly catch a person's eye, they will return your smile as, just like yawning, smiles are contagious.

CHAPTER 11
WHEN YOU'RE SMILING

" Smile , it is the key that fits the lock of everybody's heart."

Anthony J. D'Angelo

SMILES: INSTANT FACELIFTS

Life's lessons have taught me this: a smile is the number one feature that makes people attractive. It's a welcome mat. It's what makes folks approachable. People with a great smiles radiate a warmth that draws others to them instantly.

Some people naturally have a great smile. Others, analytical types like me, must work at it. One way to tell if you're in my category is to recall picking up your developed photos. As you flipped through the pictures, you didn't like the way you looked in most of them. But then...you discovered that one great picture of yourself. In it, you look friendly, you're smiling broadly and your eyes twinkle. Now THAT picture looks like you!

I hate to say it, but ALL the pictures look like you, even those you dislike. Unfortunately, those "bad" photos, where your face doesn't look its best, portray how you often appear. In fact, you might normally look even worse, since you were TRYING to look good for the camera. Usually you're not even making that effort, and may appear even less inviting than you do in "bad" photos. And if you're like me, you assume you're not particularly photogenic and that your smile needs work. When you've mastered your smile, you'll consistently look better in photos. Most important, though, you'll be more attractive and approachable every day.

When you're having a good time, does your face show it? You might be surprised. In everyday life the same concept applies. You might be enjoying your job, but fail to show it. You may want to meet someone, yet not give them a single, friendly clue. You can even be IN LOVE with somebody, and totally hide it. Your face should express what you feel when you wish to connect with others.

SMILE AEROBICS FOR EMOTIONAL HEALTH

One way to become better at smiling is increasing your awareness. Take notice of those you find warm and inviting. Is it their smile? Make an effort to LOOK for great smiles. Notice the appeal of people who smile with their EYES, not just their mouth. The whole face gets involved. Consider these people your models. Study yourself in the mirror. How do you look in the rest room, when shopping, and while passing a reflective window? Do you look friendly? Approachable? Do you really LIKE the image you're projecting?

In fact, a mirror is ideal for your smile workout. Practice various smiles toward capturing that perfect look for the camera. Work on expressing your smile with your eyes. A tip: cut a paper rectangle that permits you to see only your eyes in the mirror. Practice smiling just with your eyes. Get used to the feel of your cheekbones as they lift to brighten your eyes. When you see how a great smile LOOKS, remember how it FEELS. When you can finally project your best smile, hold it. Turn away from the mirror. How does your face feel? What muscles are you using? Make an effort to develop muscle memory, so you can instantly recreate this smile at will.

THE SMILING REMINDER

Sometimes it's life's little reminders that help us focus on making self-improvements. I set out to find a "smile" lapel pin as a permanent token of my smile's importance. After a fruitless one-year search, I commissioned the design and production of smile pins. Now when I encounter a total stranger with a million-dollar smile (not an everyday occurrence), I share the compliment, "You have a wonderful smile...thanks for brightening my day! I'd like you to have my golden smile pin." Then I might add, "And someday, when YOU see a total stranger with a fantastic smile, you can pass on the pin to them."

This little reminder has conditioned me to search out life's glowing smiles, and not to allow them to pass unnoticed. You needn't search for a smile pin to remind you. You can choose another object, like a clown pin, that will program you to focus on smile power. Or consider something that nobody else sees, like whimsical underwear. In fact, you may discover that the sheer strength of just your awareness can create positive life changes. With practice you can focus on life's smiles; and create your own relaxed, naturally warm smile. And THEN when you get back a roll of photos, you'll like almost all of them! That's certainly been my pleasant experience. And when you encounter customers, strangers, or loved ones, you'll always be ready to pass on your award-winning smile!

CHAPTER 12
BODY LANGUAGE

Body language is the most under-appreciated form of non-verbal communication. How can this be? Well the answer is rather simple. How can a person appreciate something that they do not understand or know how to utilize? Do you know who is the biggest culprit? Males! Now I am probably going to get a lot of emails telling me of how wrong this is, but it is far from this. Before you log into your email, consider one question. Which sex uses body language the most, and in all its forms? The answer is females. If they use it more often then males, then they would probably have a better eye for body language. A males main tool to initiate body language is his eyes, which are usually accompanied by subtle face gestures. This is why males tend to be better at it then females. On the other hand, females use all the forms of body language. Not to say that males don't, but it is not as common.

Women are the 'masters' of body language. The type of body language used by women depends on the personality of that individual women. Shy and quiet women usually use more subtle forms of body language, which hinders a mans ability to tell whether or not body language is being used. With these type of women, the initial reads are hard. However, if you get to know that woman, then over time comfort while remove this inability to produce readable body language. An outgoing and playful women is not subtle at all when it comes to using body language. They use it more liberally and is very easy to notice. They are very flirtatious with their non-verbal communication, and could escalate to slight caressing.

Since I mentioned it, I will briefly explain the use of a light touch. This touch sends signals up to receptors in a man's brain, which releases euphoric neurotransmitters. In doing so, the man feels a sensation of happiness, comfort, acceptance and attractiveness all in one, hence the euphoric state. The trick is that you want to leave them wanting more, therefore leave this slight caressing to a minimum. Not enough to make them drool, but not too little that they do not feel teased.

What are the main tools a women has that she uses to show body language? This question is similar to me asking someone how to determine how big a person's net worth is. The number one answers is their ASSETS. The same answer applies to women and their use of body language; however, this is far from the only thing they use. How do women use their assets? A major way is by revealing a little skin. Men go internally crazy when they see a little skin. However, everything has to be applied in moderation too. Too much revealed skin can be seen as attention craving; where as too little can be seen as being up tight. The following are a couple of ways in which women use sex appeal to show body language:

1) Body Contour

Women that normally use this have a nice, voluptuous body. They use the contours of their body to tell how they are feeling. They try to increase the arch of their body to amplify its affect on the person who she is trying to grab their attention. This is a personal favourite of mine because it shows off the natural beauty of a woman's body, similar to that of a sculpture. Why did I start with the body? Studies show that the first judgment a male passes on a female without seeing facial features is the body. Usually, if they do not like what they see then they move onto the next woman; however if they do then they move onto the other assets of the breasts and rear-end. Ladies, when I say "if they do not like what they see", this is not eluding to body type, different men have different tastes therefore if you do not fit their cirteria then they move on. My philosophy is that EACH and EVERY woman is uniquely beautiful, it just takes the right guy to discover it.

2) Body Position

Usually, if woman are self-conscious about their body, they will use what they believe is to be the best asset that they have. They may use their breast, rear-end or even legs. Now this all depends on the preference of the guy as well. Some men favour one asset over the other and can make the difference whether a man shows interest back to your body language. Woman that like to flaunt their breasts will wear low cut shirts, those that like to flaunt their rear-end will wear tighter jeans and those that like to flaunt their legs will wear a skirt of some sort. Just to prove a point, the next time you go out for lunch with some friends go to a Moxie's, Keg or some sort of bar-lounge atmosphere. Guess what all the cocktail waitress do? They flaunt all three parts mentioned above. Can you guess their main customers? MALES, what a surprise! Just a quick fact. These cocktail waitresses can make up to 5x more tips than a waitress at restaurant of equal comparison. These are crazy phenomenons, I know. This is the biggest problem I see when I help people with either their businesses or with their love lives. People look for the non-obvious, I always tell them to start with the things that they know or the things that they have in this case.

For men it is a totally different ball game. You will never see them flaunt skin unless at the beach, nor will they try to make body gestures because males bodies were not made for that. Like I stated in Part 1 of this article, men mainly use their eye language to communicate non-verbally. However, the difference here is whether or not the man has the CONFIDENCE to initiate or return non-verbal communication. Firstly, a lot of men in general lack confidence so this in itself is not surprising. I will cover confidence and how to overcome its inhibition in another article because this a whole beast by itself to tame. The main reason why men are not comfortable initiating in body language is because they are not confident in their ability to understand it or how to give it back. So they will just shy away, unless they are under the influence of alcohol which is a instant confidence booster. So ladies if a man does not show any non-verbal communication back, do not be alarmed because chances are that he has no idea what he is doing. However, if you encounter a man that does show it back but is absolutely horrible at it, give him a chance because this is easily fixable. It is easier to teach a man body language than it is to teach them how to be confident. Therefore, think of yourself as a teacher, and you are teaching your student, the man, how to conduct proper body language. As well as, it helps the man learn what to look for in the future so that they are not as clueless.

As you may have noticed I am gradually progressing towards actual initiation or what I call 'engagement' of a person that you are attracted to, whether it be to their physical appearance, or to their perceived personality. It is very important to take it step by step because a lot of people when they sell dating advice, they just tell you the "how-to", but the dating world is so volatile because as I said before every situation is unique but the patterns shown are eternal. A person selling a product would have started at the initiation of a individual. But how do you do that without first understanding out how they think and what they do to show that they are interested in you.

CHAPTER 13
UNDERSTAND BODY
LANGUAGE

Your body language says a lot about you and has a major impact on how others see you. As such you can learn a lot from the body language of others.

Body language accounts for up to 55% of how we communicate. Body language along with verbal cues can indicate a number of different things depending on the context. People with powerful body language with open movements that take up more space tend to feel more confident. They are more likely to have less stress, be more dominant, take more risks and be more optimistic. Dominant body language creates a powerful appearance. Studies show that even faking high and low poses effected the confidence level of the participants both positively and negatively.

The idea of fake it til you make it may seem false, but in faking it the process will help you become it starting with small changes to your body language. Something everyone can learn.

Here are three common situations in which body language is especially important - a job interview, dating and detecting lies, and ways to read between the lines to help understand what is really going on.

Like it or not we all lie a lot. When conversing with a stranger we are likely to lie once or more in the first 10 minutes. They may be little lies but we still do it. Most of us will participate in deception from time to time to avoid conflict, but we are probably better off telling the truth. Words can be deceptive but the human body has a hard time hiding lies. Using your own body language and being able to read body language of others can be extremely useful when communicating with others.

The Basics of Body Language:

Your primary goal when reading body language is to determine their comfort level in their current situation. There is a process of combining verbal cues and body language to determine this.

Positive body language:

- ✓ Moving or leaning closer to you

- ✓ Relaxed, uncrossed limbs

- ✓ Long periods of eye contact

- ✓ Looking down and away out of shyness

- ✓ Genuine Smiles

Negative body language:

- ➤ Moving or leaning away from you

- ➤ Crossed arms or legs

- ➤ Looking away to the side

- ➤ Feet pointed away from you, or towards an exit

- ➤ Rubbing/scratching their nose, eyes, or the back of their neck

A single cue can be misleading so it's essential to pay attention to multiple behavioral cues.

LYING:

Being able to judge whether someone is lying through reading their Body Language is a big advantage. Your intuition is never 100% accurate, but with practice you can become more aware of when you're being lied to. This technique will help with the big lies but it's very difficult to detect white lies, lies of omission or exaggeration.

Research has shown that liars often exhibit much of the uncomfortable behavior plus some specific additional traits.

Fake Smiles

Research has shown it is almost impossible to fake a genuine smile when lying. This is why many people appear awkward in family photos. The smiles look awkward if they are faking it. Your genuine smile is in the eyes as your smile pushes up your cheeks and creates wrinkles around your eyes. It is difficult to fake this as you need to feel some genuine happy emotion to do it and that is almost impossible if you are lying. So a fake smile is helpful in determining if a lie is in progress.

Too much Eye Contact and a Stiff Upper Body

Often a liar will overcompensate with too much eye contact, and appear stiff while they try not to fidget, this can make you feel uncomfortable and unsettled. In genuine conversations people move and do not hold eye contact for long periods. Liars because they are uncomfortable will often rub their neck or eyes and look away to the side and opt to do little. If you notice tense shoulders and a high amount of eye contact you likely talking to a liar..

Verbal Cues

Pay attention to the conversation, liars will offer more details and suggest punishments for the real offenders if they are being accused of something. They will answer your questions with a question giving them time to make up an answer. This type of conversation paired with negative body language points to dishonesty.

It's important to realize that some people may always behave awkwardly. Look for multiple cues and trust your instincts and ask for verification if you just aren't sure.

DATING:

On the first date understanding your date's body language is incredibly helpful in knowing when not to talk about something that makes them uncomfortable.

Basically you are just looking for general indications of comfort and discomfort. This means paying attention to how guarded their body language is. On a first date most people will be fairly guarded crossing their arms, keeping a distance and keeping their palms face upwards. Your goal is to encourage them to be more open by being more open and welcoming yourself with uncrossed arms and a warm genuine smile. We all tend to mimic the behavior of others so if you're warm and comfortable it will help them become more comfortable.

Comfort levels can fluctuate on a first date as they are nerve-wracking, and you are likely to make a few mistakes. Don't worry just keep going. Watch for positive body language and focus on what brings that out. If you witness negative body language change the subject. Of course there will be evenings when you just don't jibe with the other person and there will be many awkward periods. If this happens know that person wasn't for you and move on.

JOB INTERVIEWS:

Job interviews are similar to first dates except that on a date you are on an equal basis whereas in a job interview the interviewer has the power. This creates a situation were you are more uncomfortable than the interviewer. You could easily display negative body language which you need to override in order not to appear closed off.

First Impressions

First impressions do count so a smile, a handshake and a warm greeting along with the previously mentioned positive body language will bode you well for a comfortable interview.

Go into the interview prepared, this will increase your comfort level and add to your confidence level. To prepare research the company and any individuals that may be interviewing you.

Natural comfort is your most valuable tool, however there some tricks to help you enhance your comfort. Eye contact is important especially when asking questions and when the interviewer has something to tell you. Avoid blocking your eyes, lean slightly forward, and appear to be a good listener by placing your hand over your mouth indicating you are not going to talk and are paying attention.

Any reasonable Interviewer will understand that you are a little nervous and tense. In fact if you're overconfident it can indicate that you are not taking the interview seriously.

CHAPTER 14
STEPS TO KNOW A PERSON COMPLETELY

In our life, what is more important than knowing people who matters to us most? The number of such people may not be very high, yet they influence our lives almost completely. If we can know their minds and thoughts better, there is no doubt that we not only make our life better but also the life of the people around us. It is no secret that we can get what we want in life only by the proper understanding of the people. In our personal life, we can bring peace and happiness only by understanding our loved ones. In our professional life we can motivate our colleagues and team to achieve the goal of the organizations only by properly understanding them.

Yet understanding people is the most difficult knowledge to learn in real life. This knowledge is not taught in any school or college. Our understanding of man based on the bookish knowledge derived from the books of psychology, management, religion, culture etc. fails to help us in understanding the real life people. Which theory is to be applied on a person, when every person is different and every theory is different? Theories are much easier to use in material domain as every atom, every molecule and every material behaves in identical manner. How to deal with man, when every one is different and no two people are similar?

It gives us no respite, to know a person merely in terms of probability or statistic when the person is too important to you. You can't be satisfied to know that if you scold your children, he is 56% likely to perform poorly in exam. However, if you do not scold the child, his chances of poor performance are increased to 60%. These researches can't help you in exercising of either option. You are scared of using either option as you want your child to improve. You do not have thousands of children that you can be satisfied with a statistical probability. After all in the first case the chances of failure is 44% while in the second case, it is 40%. You have only one child and you want him to improve. You want the right solution and not a random solution.

The solution of all our problems lies in knowing the person as accurately as one knows himself. If that can be possible then you can be almost absolutely sure that you will get the desired result. Are there really such methods of knowing a person so completely?

One Person Four Personalities

We all bear many hats in our life. We are the simplest creature on earth yet the most complex human being. Who are we?

We are a different person at our home. We are so simple at our home that even our child knows us well. We play with them, enjoy the simple games and become a child itself. Our education, profession and knowledge do not seem to influence our dear ones like our children, souse, parents and even our dogs. They all seems to know us very well.

We have a different personality with our friends. They too know us well. We all know the mind of all our friends. The older is the friend; the better is our understanding of him. Friends not only know our personality but they become the integral part of our personality. After all it is wisely said "a man is known by the company he keeps". Thus, your friends are often a close refection of your personality.

Yet we are quite different on our job. The same person becomes different when performing his job. We are completely different person as a cop, philosopher, teacher, politician or a sweeper. Our actions and thoughts are shaped according to our job. There is a great similarity in all people of similar profession. All cops have similar traits, so have the traits of all teachers.

We are part of the society, nation and the world. We are affected by every thing that is happening anywhere in the society or the world. A man of India is different than a man of China or USA. A man of twenty first century is different than a man of tenth century.

However, man in not merely only a body i.e. the material entity but he also has mind, soul and spirit. The complete personality of the person can be known only by knowing his body, mind, soul and spirit. Once you know all four, there is nothing left in the person to be known as he has become your extended Self by the presence of the common spirit. The methods to know these four aspects of man have requires following four steps.

The Physical Self

The body of the person is the most obvious representation of his or her personality. Body represents the physical self of the person as an animal and represents the basic instincts or the natural instinct of the person. The first distinction in the body emerges from the sex of the person. The bodies of the males and females are as different as their basic instinct. The basic instincts of males and females are quite similar across the world. So if you know one, you know all. The second important thing which the body represents is the raw passion or sensual desire of the person. A man with uncontrolled passion would have uncontrolled, fat and disproportionate body while a man who has disciplined and controlled his desire would have a fitter and proportionate body. The movement of the body and limbs too represents the natural personality of the person. This is often called as "body language". A restless person must have a restless body and peaceful person would have a peaceful body.

The Mental Self

The mind of the person is the most important attribute in his professional life. The mind of the person is shaped on the basis of the education and experience of the person in his lifetime. One can know the mind of the person from his educational qualification, experience and profession experience as all goes into shaping the mind of the person. The mind of the person is the source of the reason and logic used by the person to interact with the world. One can also understand the mind of the person in the course of discussion and communication i.e. the way he answers or responds to your logic and reasons.

The Intellectual Self

The body, senses and mind apparently seem to be independent from each other. It is also possible to measure these attributes of human personality by suitable instruments and tests. Yet they are all controlled by the Soul of the person which represents the intelligence of the person.

The mind and body of the person are changing every moment. A person is happy in one movement but get worried on the very next moment. A person may be active in one moment but may become inactive due to illness or hunger or tiredness few moments later. Thus our assessment of the person may be totally wrong if it is based merely on the knowledge of physical and mental self. We have to know the force behind the body and mind which does not change.

The real nature of the person is intelligence of the person. Body and mind are merely the tools in the control of the intelligence self. Just like a fire can be used to cook food or burn people, so does the body and mind can be used for good or bad purposes by the intelligence? The intelligence of the person has to be understood by the synthesis of the diverse traits and actions of the personality of the person using our own intelligence and reasoning.

The Spiritual Self

It is believed in scriptures and philosophies that every living being has the spark of the God or Spirit. No person is, therefore, independent from other beings as everyone is connected by the common thread of this spirit. It is due to the common spirit that we cry when we see people in misery and fell happy when give happiness to others. It is due to the spiritual self, that we connect ourselves with the rest of the world and enjoys or feel pain in our life.

The spiritual self of the person is the non-material aspect of the human personality. It is best known to our loved ones, when there are no material rewards or punishment for our actions. In your home, you get no reward or punishment in being nice or nasty to your children, your wife or your parents and elders. Yet the expression of our spiritual self is the sour of all our happiness and pain.

A spiritual person, therefore, highly value the nonmaterial realities of life and seek happiness in selfless activities. We are all spiritual to some extent else we can never get happiness in our life. If you donate one billion dollars to your computer or a lathe machine, it can never feel any happiness. Only a man can feel happiness even by wealth since he can use the wealth for distribution to others selflessly which , makes him and others happy.

The understanding of the spiritual self is purely based on intuition and requires no knowledge or reasoning. It is similar to the understanding that a child or a dog has to their parents or their master. The sign of spirituality is the peace, love and happiness. So when you meet a person and feel more peaceful, loving and happy, the person must be highly spiritual. You can therefore expect help and compassion from such person. If the feeling is otherwise, you have met a materialistic and devilish person, who can only seek material favour from you or seek pleasure in your pain.

The Complete Knowledge of A Person

Only by knowing all four aspect of a person which represents the body, mind, soul and spirit of the person, you can understand the real person. Such understanding of a person requires not only the logical mind but also the use of your basic instinct , intelligence , intuition and experience. You can then know the complete person using your intuition and know the real thoughts of the person. Once you have understood the thoughts and soul of a person, what is left unknown about the person.

CHAPTER 15
HOW THE BRAIN PROCESSES
THOUGHT

Have you ever looked at a newborn and wondered what they could possibly be thinking? Since there is no language yet in their head, how does their brain process what it is seeing, hearing and feeling?

Learning is about the brain forming millions of such beliefs, sometimes great beliefs that serve you well your whole life, other times wrong interpretations that haunt you well into your adult life.

Take this, for example. As a newborn, perhaps only a few days old, the baby cries and instantly the mother tenderly nurtures the baby and smiles. The baby forms a new belief, "I am loved." That will certainly be a useful belief all through out the baby's life.

Baby number two cries and mother is trying to cook supper and is preoccupied with the stresses of daily life. She does love the baby very much, yet when she picks the baby up, there is stress in her voice, and perhaps she is not as nurturing as usual. The baby forms a new belief, "I am not loved." That will surely make life harder for the baby as it grows up.

With these two examples, its important to note that the brain doesn't always draw the correct conclusions, in fact, its impossible to draw the right conclusions because there isn't enough information or life experience. The baby can't possible comprehend what mother number two is going through, yet it must interpret the reaction.

Often, the baby draws the wrong conclusion. A basic belief is formed and all beliefs are drawn around the erroneous conclusion.

Does this explain how two children can grow up with the same parents, in the same town and have the same experiences, and one child will believe "My dad was a jerk." and the other child will believe "My dad was a great dad." Its all your interpretation of life from infancy. Scary, don't you think?

The beliefs that are formed in infancy then affect our whole life.

MYTHS ABOUT THE BRAIN

The brain is one of all the foremost superb organs in the human body. It controls the central nervous system, and helps us in taking respiration, thinking, talking and walking. The brain is additionally unbelievably complicated organ, comprising around one hundred billion neurons. There is a lot going on with the brain that there are several completely different fields of medication and science dedicated to treating and studying it, including neurology, that treats physical disorders of the brain; psychology - the study of behavior and mental processes; and psychological medicine, that treats mental disorders. Some aspects of each tend to overlap, and alternative fields cross into study of the brain further.

Myths regarding the brain are especially difficult to jest at, since the brain is not completely understood. However, over the past few decades, many scientists have done enough research to discredit a few widespread brain myths. In the research, scientists found the facts on brain and psychological feature, brain and its behavior, how the brain interfaces with specific subject-area information and motivation was given, including clarifications on common myths regarding the brain were given.

We have several myths regarding the brain, however only a few certainties. Some of the authors dispel common myths about the brain and make available comprehensive, valuable information of how it works.

By combining latest analysis and religious insights, demolishing the 5 most widespread myths about the brain that limit our potential, and then showing the strategies to:

> Create the best lifestyle for a healthy brain

> Promote happiness and well-being through the

mind-body connection

➢ Overcome the foremost common challenges, like state of mind, depression, anxiety, and obesity

➢ Reduce the risks of aging

➢ Use your brain rather than letting it use you

Our brain is capable of inconceivable healing and constant reshaping. Actually, though, the living, pulsing brain residing in our bone is not just an uninteresting dull, bland grey; it is also white, black and red. Like several myths regarding the brain, this one incorporates a grain of truth.

The good news is there's an entire new generation of physicians and researchers that are debunking recent myths about the brain, and giving us the tremendous new insights into functioning of the brain. Finally, one of all the foremost vital myths regarding the brain and aging is that everything changes within the brain and mental functioning is unhealthy. An important line of research analysis in psychological feature aging shows that some mental functions completely differ with age.

CHAPTER 16
HOW THE BRAIN LEARNS

How the brain learns is a subject that still requires a lot of study. What scientists do know is that the learning process of the brain is dependent on how it is able to make connections among the brain cells. That may be a simple explanation on how the complex brain functions as it tries to learn through a variety of stimuli.

How the brain learns can be associated by how it is able to create memories. It is through the connections that it can make that lead to the creation of memories and facilitation of the learning process.

The basics of the process begin with the neurons in the brain. A neuron is a nerve cell that receives information coming from the sensory organs and then transmits that information to the other nerve cells.

Some of these neurons transmit the different information that it receives to other parts of the body that also interacts with the environment.

The connections established from which information passes from one neuron to another are called synapses. The different levels of information that the neurons receive from the synapses that they have established determine the output information that it sends out. This seems to create a sort of wiring diagram that enables different neurons to send and receive information from one another.

The number of synapses among neurons is at its minimum during the development process of the baby in the womb. After birth, it gains about two thirds of its adult size just after birth.

After that, the rest of the synapses are formed after birth with a part of this established as humans go through different stimuli in life. These synapses are said to explain how the brain learns. The neurons seem to establish a large number of synapses between them right after birth.

The scientists believe that the synapse overproduction is due to the fact that some of these connections are later on lost or disappear. This may allow the neurons to select and establish appropriate connections, and disregard the inappropriate ones to create more efficient connections with each other. This is how the brain learns.

HOW THE BRAIN FUNCTIONS TO LEARN NEW SKILLS

The way science, sports, and education approach learning new skills does not follow the way our brain works. Science now knows the brain is a complex neurological organism that rewires itself as it learns and refines skills, but the science of how the brain learns has not been integrated into the lexicon yet.

Academia teaches as if the conscious, thinking part of the brain can learn by itself. The thinking part of the brain evolved after the older, sensory brain.

All input to the thinking brain comes from the sensory brain. In fact, the sensory brain processes millions of bits of information in any given moment, but sends just a fraction of that data (16 - 40 bits) to the thinking brain.

The sensory brain receives its information from the body, through the senses: what we hear, see, touch, taste, smell, and what touches us.

How are the senses activated? By movement. Science confirms all information the brain processes is through movement. Some neuroscientists such as Daniel Wolpert Ph.D. go so far as to say the only reason the brain exists is because we move.

Neuroscientists such as Michael Merzenich, Ph.D. have studied the correlation of movement with how we think. In one experiment he showed that as a skill is learned fewer irrelevant parts of the body are used, and that as the movements become more precise and refined, neurons fire faster. He further showed that the faster neurons fire, the faster we think. Another important study Merzenich conducted showed that our ability to think more clearly directly correlates with the quality of our movements.

How do we determine the quality of our movements? Science identifies which muscles should be used during a movement such as a golf swing. Sports and exercise focus on which muscles to use during an activity as well. The problem is if you are using the correct muscles to perform an action you feel nothing. Why would your brain need to let you know if you are using the "right"muscles? The focus should be on what muscles you feel and whether you are limited in some way during an action. Feeling the burn is your brain sending alarm signals to stop doing the movement in the same way. When you feel stiff, sore, discomfort, or pain your brain is telling you to change the way you are moving.

Science and sports/fitness focus on isolated parts of the body such as just using the biceps in a weight-training curl. The brain is concerned about how the entire structure is balancing through every movement such that the body is constantly adjusting. In addition every movement should travel through the structure such that no movement is isolated to a particular component (such as a lower arm). Great rock climbers know that to estab-lish an effective hand hold they must be relaxed through the wrist, elbow and shoulder joint to allow the rest of the body to support the hold. Doing isolated movements to strengthen some parts of the body may unintentionally cause limitations to a particular skill. Every activity you do should be about how your entire body moves within it.

Optimal function within a movement is when you are in the zone. The zone is defined as the state of being when you function optimally, your body and mind are inseparable, any activity you do is effortless and timeless, and you move without conscious oversight.

CHAPTER 17
DOES MEMORY RESIDE
INSIDE THE BRAIN?

On Jun 2, 2005, NBC Philadelphia had an interesting report. Christina Santhouse had caught a virus that caused a rare brain disorder known as Rasmussen's Syndrome at an age of 8. And her doctor had to perform hemispherectomy, removal of half of the brain, on her. After 10 years, Christina was about to graduate from high school with honors. After the surgery, she had a slight limp and her left hand didn't work at all. She had also lost her peripheral vision, but otherwise, she was an ordinary teen. A similar case was reported on Telegraph (UK) on May 29, 2002, a girl named Bursa had the same disorder and her left brain was removed when she was 3, she became fluent in Dutch and Turkish when she was 7. In 1987, A. Smith reported that one patient with hemispherectomy had completed college, attended graduate school and scored above average on intelligence tests. Studies have found no significant long-term effects on memory, personality, or humor after the procedure, and minimal changes in cognitive function overall.

The outcome of hemispherectomy is surprising. Neuroscience tends to suggest memory is stored in the neurons in the brain. If that premise stands true, removing half of the brain would destroy one's memory if memory is stored in the network structure of neurons as one school of cognitive physiology suggests, or at least destroy half of the memory if bits of memory information are stored in individual neurons in the brain as suggested by another school of cognitive neuroscience. But it is apparent that the results disagree with either of the explanations. Removing part of the brain has been one of the standard surgical operations for severe epilepsy and has been performed thousands of times. Many of the results are quite similar to those of hemispherectomy.

The orthodox explanation for the observation is that information stored in the infected brain areas is duplicated in the health part of the brain prior to the surgery. This rationalization is still inadequate when you take into account how a brain surgery is performed. Surgeon has to remove the infected area and some surrounding health tissue, sometimes a much larger tissue than the infected area, to make sure infection does not spread. If the information stored in the infected areas is reproduced somewhere in the brain before surgical procedure, some information is still lost when surrounding health brain tissue is removed, consequently the memory would suffer.

This is not observed after the surgery. So it is necessary to assume that the memory stored in the neighboring health tissue is also replicated in other parts of the brain. This raises a question: how does the brain know how much health tissue is going to be taken out? If the brain does not know, surgeries will inevitable destruct part of the memory. The belief that memory is stored in the brain (in neurons or in the network of neurons) apparently contradicts with findings in brain surgeries.

In the 1920s Karl Lashley conducted a series of experiments trying to identify which part of the brain memories are stored. He trained rats to find their way through a maze, and then made lesions in different parts of the cerebral cortex in an attempt to erase its original memory trace. His experimental animals were still able to find their way through the maze no matter where he put lesions on their brains. He therefore concluded that memories are not stored in any single area of the brain, but are instead distributed throughout it. Distributing the memory of every single event over the whole brain is energetically inefficient and mathematically impossible. If his reasoning is not confined to the brain, the logical conclusion should be that memory is not stored in the brain.

Instincts are obviously inherited and nobody has any slight idea where the information making up the instincts is stored, and cognitive memory is thought to be acquired through experience and stored by changing the signal chemicals in the neurons in the brain.

New research reveals that even cognitive memory can be inherited. A study by Larry Feig at Tufts University School of Medicine in Boston indicates that mother mice that receive mental training before they become pregnant can pass on their cognitive benefits to their young even there is no direct contact among the mothers and their offspring. It is obvious that the cognitive memory is not acquired by the young through experience, and there is no apparent way for the young to store the information in their neurons, then where do the young retrieve the memory from? Maybe from where they store their instincts information, a place nobody knows yet.

"Brain areas such as the hippocampus, the amygdala, the striatum, or the mammillary bodies are thought to be involved in specific types of memory. For example, the hippocampus is believed to be involved in spatial learning and declarative learning, while the amygdala is thought to be involved in emotional memory. Damage to certain areas in patients and animal models and subsequent memory deficits is a primary source of information. However, rather than implicating a specific area, it could be that damage to a pathway traveling through the area is actually responsible for the observed deficit" If one stores all his possessions in a warehouse connected to his house through a highway, he would not be able to get anything from the warehouse if the highway is broken down. To infer that everything is stored on the highway based on the facts he can not get anything when the highway is interrupted is ridiculous. Even the connection between the brain and memory is well established, it is beyond logic to conclude that memory reside inside the brain.

CHAPTER 18
STRATEGIES FOR EFFECTIVE READING

Regular reading is essential for anyone. It will help one to develop his/her knowledge, skills or attitude. It is often done for different purposes by different groups of people. Some read for advancing their knowledge; some others do it for improving their language skills; another section of people do it just for pleasure. Whatever be the purpose, the habit helps everyone in improving his/her personality in many ways.

Students and academics usually pay little attention to assess how bad they read. They do not, in normal case, assess how well they can improve the speed of their reading. Speed of one's reading can lead to improvement in learning effectiveness. Learning to read well is an essential skill every academic should develop systematically.

The reading habit helps everyone build up his/her personality in many ways. Choosing the right text or material to read is the first thing. Reading for academic purposes is strenuous. Students need to focus on understanding the contents of the material in depth. But reading for pleasure tends to be light. The latter does require less concentration and can be done at an average speed of 100-200 words per minute. Prior knowledge of the subject is a key element of effective reading comprehension.

There is a practice for some people to read word by word. It is better to focus on reading phrases rather than just words while reading. Reading the material as phrases allows one's brain to process the reading input as 'ideas or phrases'.

Reading Strategies

There are different types of techniques for reading. For improving the rate, one should practice skimming, scanning or previewing as a reading strategy. The method should be chosen as the reading material and purpose demand.

The first one is skimming. It is reading rapidly for gathering the main points. In this process, the reader reads quickly to gain a general idea. The reader understands the whole text without reading it from first to last or word to word. The technique may allow you to read up to 1000 words a minute. In this process, the key ideas of a text is gathered by reading first and last paragraphs, topic sentences, and other parts like titles, abstracts, summary of chapters, photograph captions, etc.

In skimming, the practice is to identify whether to read

or not, what to read carefully, and which place is the right one to begin with. If you skim through a text before you read it, it will help you understand the material better.

In scanning, the practice is to read rapidly to find out a specific piece of information. It is a technique that anyone can employ to find out specific information, facts or ideas without reading the whole text. Scanning may help you examine up to 1,500 words a minute. The purpose of scanning a text is to evaluate the relevance of the material. Scanning is to be done before skimming. It will help you determine whether a material carries the information the reader wants. Once a resource is scanned, it can then be skimmed for further details.

Surface reading is yet another process of reading. It is used to find the 'information words' from the text you read. Half of the words in a material are "information" words. They alone make sense of the material. The other words in it works like glue and paint. They provide connections but are not essential for making out the meaning. Concentrating on information words may help you read faster. The comprehension will also be better. Paying more attention to what the author is trying to say is the essence of this type of reading.

Extensive reading is reading a longer text, often for pleasure with emphasis on overall meaning. But intensive reading is reading a short text for detailed information.

Phrase reading is yet another process.

Process of Rapid Reading

The process of reading results in a series of eye jerks, known as 'fixations'. During fixations, the eyes take in words for comprehension. Slow readers take in only one or two words in each fixation. Increase the words in each fixation by continuous practice. You will be able to gather more number of words in each fixation. Therefore, you have to practise reading the sentences without eye jerks, but with smooth movement of eyes from one to another. One can practice this strategy with conscious effort.

Marking important points in the text is good for learning. Underlining or highlighting key words, and making notes in margins etc., can improve speed in reading. Making marks in texts such as underlining the sentences can help you in improving concentration, in identifying key points and in making the book easier to survey, if you prefer to do so.

Other Points to Remember

Note taking always supports reading comprehension. Taking down essential points is what you do in note taking. Note-taking during reading or listening can help you gain deeper understanding and reflection of the text you read. It can help you remember or recollect easily what you have read. Summarizing what the reader has learned is another way to improve their overall comprehension of text.

Language proficiency will help you read better. Reading, on the other hand, will help your proficiency in language skills. Mastering the basic 3,000 or more words, which constitute approximately 80 percent of texts in English you normally use, can aid you in reading, understanding and learning any material on any subject in English, easily. Extensive reading, comprehension skills, reading fluency, and vocabulary building, are all integral ingredients of advancement of knowledge.

Active readers, with clear goals for reading, can become good learners. They regularly evaluate whether the text and their reading practice meet their goals. Good readers scan the text before they read. They get to know what the structure of the text is and what sections of the text are relevant to them. Good readers can make predictions about what is to come. They choose what to read carefully, what to read quickly, what to re-read, what not to read, and so on. Good readers read different texts differently. They evaluate the text's quality and value, and respond to the text intelligently.

DIFFERENT TECHNIQUES TO IMPROVE READING COMPREHENSION

When kids are first learning to read, we teach them their letters, the sounds associated with those letters, which we call phonemic awareness and in many cases we teach words as whole units or sight words. Soon sentence structure is taught and increasingly more complex sentences are introduced. During this process, kids are grasping these lessons at many different levels and mastering these skills at varying paces. The teaching continues on. Before long, reading becomes a means to an end.

Students are expected to read and extract meaning. They have transitioned from learning to read to reading to learn. For many this transition is effortless and happens organically. However, some students require a bit more intentional training and still others need the process of comprehension completely revealed to them.

I believe many of our struggling students need this process to be explicitly taught and that is why so many do not have either the ability to comprehend or any interest in reading. Therefore, they quite rapidly lose pace with their peers and fall critically behind.

However, there is even more I believe effects our student's previous successes and current struggles.

To further ensure success, we must know our students and how they learn best. Simply speaking, we must know whether they are auditory, visual, tactile, or kinesthetic learners. This can be assessed with any number of free online assessments. The information can be as eye opening for the student as the teacher. It is a great beginning of the year activity. Once this information has been discovered, the teacher can tailor his or her teaching to meet the needs of all students.

Another important bit of information is knowing their learning history. We must know how they see themselves as a reader. As a learner.

Each of our students comes to us with a school history. The experiences they have had have begun to create their view of themselves as learners. This can either contribute to an increased self- confidence or a confirmation of incompetence.

Knowing this information will allow us to provide our students with either challenging reading comprehension texts and activities or activities and texts geared towards building confidence.

Often teachers get so bogged down with the pressures on them to get struggling kids up to speed that we forget the child.

I believe by assessing their school history, opinion of themselves as learners and their learning styles, we can then proceed with a systematic informed and student-centered approach.

Once these assessments have been completed, students are ready to be shown how to take the words on the page and extract meaning. That is where teaching the six reading comprehension strategies come into play. Different techniques can be used to reach each student and present the strategies in a way that each student can experience success.

Presenting the six strategies must be done with care, preparation and a lot of modeling. This will also help all students slowly begin to understand the extensive internal dialogue that takes place when all good readers read.

CHAPTER 19
EXERCISES TO INCREASE YOUR READING COMPREHENSION

There are a number of activities you can do to increase your comprehension while working on building your Speed and Comprehension. Lets discuss two of them in the following paragraphs.

Speed and Comprehension: How To Improve Your Vocabulary

Here is the first activity to help you with your comprehension of your selected subject, you need to improve your vocabulary regarding that subject. When you find a word you don't understand you should look it up IMMEDIATELY, then commit it to memory by using a funny visual mnemonic. There are flashcards you can get online, for free, that have words and definitions on them for pretty much any subject you can name, using them will improve your vocabulary and that of course improves your comprehension. The simplest way maybe just to read a dictionary, however that lacks a certain focus.

Speed and Comprehension: Change Your Brainwaves

Your brain operates in states of physiological arousal called brainwave states, changing them is an important activity to boosting speed and comprehension. Generally when we are up and about our minds are in Beta state, focusing on the here and now, and what is preying on our minds. For many parts of your life this is wonderful, but not when you are trying to understand something you are reading. If you want to have a real impact on improving your comprehension you need to be able to have your brain reach the Alpha state. This can be accomplished by sitting quietly, closing your eyes, and taking deep and slow breaths. If you meditate and use a mantra such as "oooooohmmmm" you will be able to reach an alpha state much like many eastern monks do. When you feel you have reached a light trance, then begin your reading. While in this state, studies have shown that you can triple your reading speed and your comprehension. For those who don't want to meditate or practice getting into Alpha by feeling it, you can always get an EEG machine to monitor your brainwaves in real-time so you'll know when you're in Alpha. The trans-dermal electro-brain stimulator is another option to reach an alpha state, it clips on your ears and delivers a weak electrical signal that tricks your brain into an Alpha state. Finally you can also use stereo headphones and get sound mp3s or CDs that have tracks called binaural beats, that when you play them through headphones, will also eventually trick your brain into going (and staying) in Alpha. Watch your comprehension soar when you give these ideas a try!

CHAPTER 20
TIPS AND SUGGESTIONS ON MEMORIZATION AND MEMORY RECALL

Have you ever had problems remembering a phone number you looked up in a phone book or using an on line search? Do you have to write a number down to make sure you dial it correctly?

Maybe you think you have a poor memory, or that you are losing your mental acuity. I say- maybe not.

There are a range of things that have a large influence on your ability to remember in the short term.

Common factors affecting memory

A common destroyer of short term memory (and long term memory) is chronic stress and/or poor sleep (these often go together). You need to be fresh and alert for good memory. A tired stressed brain struggles to focus and to process information. If you de-stress and get plenty of sleep you will find that more than your memory will improve.

Another reason people may have poor short term memory is that they have busy minds.

Perhaps you are always thinking. When you put your keys down, and you are thinking about something else (perhaps an idea, or work troubles), your short term memory of where you placed the keys is very poorly primed.

A poorly primed short term memory means that you have little chance of forming a longer term memory of where you placed the keys. And the consequence is that you then have to go through the house to find where you left those keys.

Developing coping habits is a common technique to circumvent the "lost keys" problem.

No doubt, if you have been on this planet for a few years, you have developed a habit of putting essential things such as keys, wallet or purse, and phone in one or a small number of places. Even when you are busy or preoccupied, you can put these items in the usual place under automatic pilot. That way, you can nearly always find them quickly.

An alternative or addition to developing coping habits is to pay attention to where you place an object. Repeat in your mind the words "I placed the keys on the coffee table". Then as you walk away, visualize where you placed the keys. Focus and attention help prime short term memory for long term storage (as does emotion- but that is another article).

But- how do you remember longish numbers in the short term?

Focus- stop thinking about other things (e.g. what you are going to say to the person you are calling)

Avoid distraction

Read the numbers, then close your eyes and recall them by saying them out loud, then check it was correct

Use rhythm when saying and recalling the number (e.g. dit dit dit, dah dah dah. dit dit dit, dah)

Break longer numbers into 3 digit chunks (with a remainder chunk of 1 or 2 if needed).

Why do these things help?

Focus helps raise the importance of an action or item in your brain. This helps prime memory.

Repetition and the act of recalling both help prime memory, even in the shorter term. (Your brain locks in repeated events for easy retrieval as it has evolved to efficiently process repeated events. It sure is better than learning a much repeated process over and over again).

Rhythm is one of the tricks used by many people with amazing memory abilities.

However, I have not found a great deal of research on how this works. But it does make a useful difference for most people when it comes to remembering numbers. In essence, you are remembering them by their sound and cadence, not their meaning!

Saying the numbers out loud places the numbers into your auditory memory.

Temporary auditory memory lingers longer in the memory than temporary visual memory. Our brains probably evolved with longer retention of sounds in memory to help with mental processing of speech.

Why do we need to remember things?

Isn't that what PDAs and cutting and pasting is for?

I'll answer with one simple reason. You need a good short term memory even for simple things like understanding someone speaking a sentence, and even for speaking an unhesitating and well crafted sentence yourself.

One major learning difficulty is related to poor auditory short term memory. So, why not muscle up your short term memory by using it and improving it.

How to Improve Your Memory

Many people find it difficult to recall events that happened during their day. They describe it as a "blur" or how the day "went by so fast". This is nothing more than a less than stellar memory that can be tweaked very easily.

Many people also have trouble being able to remember figures, phone numbers, and people's names. As a person gets older the memory will naturally deteriorate. Many people view having a weak memory as having a problem.

Mnemonics are very effective tool used by the imagination to store large amounts of information. Not only can information be stored in large quantities, but it is stored efficiently and very quickly. The more one practices effective methods to improve their memory, the more of a reverberating, wave like it has in the long run.

Have you also noticed that you seem to be forgetting things more often lately? Perhaps names of people you have known for years...and you know that you know their name...but you just can't remember it? You walk from one room to another to get something and by the time you get there, you have forgotten what you went after? Frustrating, isn't it?

Do you frequently walk into a room and forget why you were going there? Some of us have problems with remembering names and faces. The ability to do well on tests or promotional exams often hinges on the ability to retain and then recall information. Despite its importance, how to improve memory is a topic that is often overlooked in our education.

Memory can be broken down into some basic components: imprint, retention and recall. Imprint is when we encounter a new piece of information that we would like to store in the memory banks. Retention is the degree to which this information creates a memorable and lasting impression or not. Finally, recall is the ability to retrieve the retained information at will. Any of these three phases can be the culprit in a memory lapse.

Do you have to be frustrated by forgetting things or are there ways to improve your memory...or at least make living with yourself less frustrating? Try some of the following tips on how to improve your memory and see if they don't make life more manageable:

Use the alarm on your watch or cell phone or smart phone. When you must be somewhere at a certain time, set the alarm to remind you to get ready to go...allow enough time to shower, do your hair and make-up/shave, change clothes, eat lunch, travel, park, and walk in to your destination with time to spare. If you find you are forgetting some of the steps in between, set an alarm for each step of the way.

Find activities that work your memory. Play games that require recall. Crossword puzzles, sudoku, logic games, mental exercises of any kind.

Make lists. If you are a paper and pen/pencil sort of person, make a list of things to do today, groceries to buy, bills to pay, phone calls to make, phone numbers you need to have handy. Post the lists in plain sight...so you do not have to remember where you put it. On the refrigerator, by the door, beside your bed, on the driver seat of your car, on your chair at work, on the mirror of the bathroom...wherever you will see the list in the course of moving through your day.

If you like electronics, you have to have a trigger to remind you to check your cell phone/PDA/smart phone so that you remember to look at the lists you have made. Put the electronic device in a place where you have to move it to do something you always do...such as on the closed toilet seat lid or in the seat where you always sit.

Follow a routine every time you do certain things. For example, always, always, always place your key ring in the same place every single time you let go of it at home...on a certain hook, in a certain dish on the hall table, in a certain pocket of your jacket or purse...you get the idea.

Practice things you have memorized in the past. Did you memorize lines for a play in high school, or the 66 books of the Bible, or the names and functions of the 12 cranial nerves, multiplication tables, or all the words to all the verses of the national anthem? Run through them again. Dust off the cobwebs and see if you can retrieve that information from your memory.

It will help you to realize that you still do remember things...even if you can't tell me what you have eaten for lunch today...or whether you even ate lunch at all.

Keep a good attitude and learn to laugh about it. Realize that a certain amount of forgetting is normal.

Here are also some tips that can help you improve memory.

Pay Attention. Sometimes people blame their recall abilities when a given fact escapes them when really the error occurred during the imprint phase. If you are not paying attention, chances are you will not remember. Part of the problem is that we are continually bombarded by trivial messages courtesy of the mass media. Attention follows interest, if something is important to remember, remind yourself of that at that time.

Make Associations. Neurologists tell us that the individual brain cells actually make physical connections with other brain cells in response to new associations. The more associations you make with a piece of information, the more likely it will be retained. Just met someone named Richard and you want to be sure you remember his name? It would be pretty hard to forget if you created a mental image of Richard Nixon putting his arm around this new acquaintance while he said, "I am not a crook, and my friend Richard here isn't here either!" The more colorful and comical an association is, the more easily it will be retained.

Get Enough Rest. Sleep deprivation and fatigue are

proven to dampen all phases of memory. Elite military units intentionally create conditions of mental and physical exhaustion during the training and selection of new recruits to see if they can function properly under those circumstances, many cannot and are dropped from the program. Memory problems are one of the early warning signs that stress has gotten out of hand. Make sure you are getting plenty of sleep, rest and recreation.

Stay Hydrated and Oxygenated. All of the organs of the body require copious amounts of water and oxygen to function at their best, especially the brain. Many of the health problems encountered the elderly are due to dehydration, including memory lapse. The brain uses a lion's share of the oxygen brought into the body. Make sure your living and work spaces are well-ventilated. Deep breathing exercises as taught in yoga can also improve memory and mind power.

Watch Out for Negative Beliefs. A person gets to a certain age and it is almost inevitable he will begin to complain about the memory starting to get foggy. This is not to say that dementia and Alzheimer's disease are not real maladies. However, the power of self-suggestion can impair memory in an otherwise healthy person.

A popular routine amongst stage hypnotists is to suggest to a receptive volunteer, "in a moment the number between 6 and 8 will disappear, you will try very hard to remember it, but it will remain a blank until I snap my fingers." Lo and behold the number does seem disappear for awhile, where the otherwise intelligent person cannot answer "what is four plus three?" The volunteer still has a perfectly fine brain, the power of belief just created a temporary and amusing memory lapse. Use positive affirmations like "my memory and mind-power grow stronger each and every day" to combat negative thoughts and beliefs.

There is another good news; you can improve your memory. This is especially true if you are younger in age. The suggestions below are very good ideas and they can actually help you to strengthen your memory

1. First, comprehend the information. This is your first look at the information given to you. Remain focused. Let your mind completely process the information. Open your mind and allow it to absorb all the facts and figures that it possible can.

2. Try to take the information and relate it to something that you are familiar with already. The ability to use this association technique is very helpful. Try to interconnect things that you can deeply relate to with the information that you need to remember. It does not have to be things that are even relevant to each other. You are just simply trying to give your brain the ability to recall

information when you think of that "trigger".

3. Repeat the information in your mind. Now, it is time to begin using your memory. After taking in the information and relating each separate item to something, start trying to recall each of them in the correct order in your mind. Keep doing this until you get all the information correctly in the right order.

4. Take a break for a few minutes and attempt to recall the information again. Then clear your mind for three or four minutes and try recalling it one more time. Even if you are able to do this accurately keep doing this drill at least three more times. Give yourself another few minutes, and then try recalling again. If you are still able to recite the information after the third time, you can be assured that the information is now stored in your brain's long-term memory.

5. Repeat these steps over until you can remember the information on your own. If you are unsuccessful at recalling all the information given to you after the few minute break, go back and repeat step one. Keep repeating each step until you can completely and accurately remember every single piece of information given to you.

These are a few relatively quick and easy suggestions that will help you stimulate your mind and increase your memory. It is okay if you don't succeed the first few times. Just use these tips regularly whenever you need help to memorize important information.

Then, keep an eye on yourself. After a few attempts, you will see that you are now taking less time to remember the information given to you. You will be stunned at how quickly you can improve your memory's ability to recall information quickly and accurately.

Lets take a look at some other tricks to improve your memory.

Remembering is one significant skill in any individual that needs to be always honed and sharpened. With a good memory, you are always able to remember things like dates, names, currency figures and many other finer details. However, a poor remembrance habit is normally embarrassing especially in public and can lead to situations like low self-esteem. Therefore, you always need to look for ways in which you can enhance your memory so that you can avoid such life-dreaded circumstances. On that note, in the following discussion, we are going to look at 15 tricks to improve your memory.

1.   Eat Right and Be Healthy

Our modern lifestyle has a few adverse effects on the power of our memories. From food habits to enormous stress and avoiding proper rest - all these play detrimental roles to improving memory. This is the reason it is of paramount importance to lead a healthy life with quality food habits.

It's on record that eating foods and supplements that contain flavonoids such as berries, grapes, tea leaves, hops, cocoa beans and vitamin D greatly boosts the neurons in the brain in the sense that they are able to form fresh memories. Additionally, these foods normally associate with enzymes and proteins that are significant for the memory and, even more importantly, help in the formation of new neurons and the crucially sufficient flow of oxygen into the brain. The anti-inflammatory and antioxidant properties of vitamin D helps to maintain healthy brain functions.

So, if you are keen to develop your memory, you must restrain yourself from junk foods and alcohol. Moreover, just like the body, the brain also needs sound rest to work at its utmost potential. As far as foods are concerned, you need to include fruits and green vegetables in your daily diet that supply the needed antioxidants to protect the brain cells from getting damaged.

2. Avoid Sugar

Sweet dishes are common weakness for many and if you are one of them, you may find it sad to know that intaking refined sugar more than the recommended limit can be harmful for your memory. Let's find out how sugar can affect the memory.

There is a significant amount of data to indicate that a high intake of refined sugar into the body of a human being has a detrimental effect on the brain and memory health. Many people consume in a day about double the amount of sugar calories recommended by the medical experts. Refined sugar leads to difficulties in forming new memories, depression, and a reduction in the brain functions. Refined sugar minimizes the production of Brain-Derived Neurotrophic Factor (BDNF) which is a very crucial element when it comes to learning and creating new memories.

3. Drink Caffeine

Caffeine has a positive effect on the memory relative to taking other substances. However, this must be done carefully to avoid habitual consumption. After consuming coffee, several cognitive tasks are carried out and in the final analyses drinking caffeine enhances the memory of a human being.

Adding to that, green tea also has a very positive role to play when it comes to improving the memory. It contains polyphenols, a powerful antioxidant that prevents free radicals from damaging the brain cells. Moreover, regular consumption of green tea is the best guide to improve memory and mental alertness and it can significantly slow the brain-aging process.

4. Exercise Your Brain

Appropriate brain exercises can help keeping your brain active through ages. Just like the muscles of the body, our brain, too, needs food and exercise of its own type. There are certain exercises that help in evolving the functionality of the brain and the power of memory. You can consider them as these are the best memory improving tricks. Moreover, if you keep on practicing these exercises over a long period of time, it's going to bring some miraculous results for you.

There are several ways in which you can exercise your brain to improve it. Some of these include reading as much as you can, increasing your vocabulary, learning new languages, writing something, post problem solving and turning off the television. With these activities you can exercise your brain and, more importantly, expand your memory, thus improving it.

5. Exercise Daily

It is said that "to achieve something you never had, you must do something you never did".

In today's busy world health is the most neglected aspect of our lives whereas, it should be the other way around! We must manage at least half an hour everyday to devote to our health. Daily exercise has multiple physical and mental benefits to offer and undoubtedly, when it's about improving the memory power, one can receive splendid results through this process.

Daily exercise can immensely enhance your brain and thinking skills. This is achieved through indirect and direct means. Through direct means, it acts on the body by stimulating physiological changes such as inflammation and reductions in insulin resistance as well as encouraging production of growth factors. It directly works on your brain by improving your sleep and mood. Through this, it's crystal-clear that consistent daily exercise is a great recipe for the improvement of your memory.

6. No Multitasking

It sounds great to have a title of "multitasking" but, do you want to know that what type of impact it has on your brain? While we are discussing about how to improve the brain's memory, you may get disappointed to know that multitasking is not helpful in improving your brain's memory.

Many times, multitasking has been termed as a counterproductive and exhaustive process. An average and perfectly working mind prefers shifting from one task to another instead of multitasking. Therefore, the exhaustive nature of multitasking, does not in anyway, improve the nature of your memory.

Various studies have already suggested that it not just causes a lack of concentration, it might slow down the work process and cause errors! If you are trying to complete 3-4 tasks by a certain point of time, you better put attention on the individual tasks because it will take much less time to complete than all the tasks being performed together. This is why it is one of the best tips to improving memory.

7. Sleep Well

After a long day of work, our body needs sound sleep at night and this is also important to stabilize the functionality of the brain. The brain performs thousands of activities throughout the day and a good sleep of 6-8 hours stabilizes the brain and puts it into the best working condition the next morning. On the contrary, not having proper sleep in the night will make you drowsy for the entire day and you will not be able to concentrate on anything.

A good amount and quality of sleep activates brain changes aiding in memory improvement. When you are asleep brain tasks can be executed accurately and quickly and with less anxiety and pressure. This is basically a recipe for boosting the capacity of your memory.

A study conducted amongst children suggests that when kids take naps between learning lessons and testing them in real life, they are very likely to perform better. It helps the process of brain growth (called neuroplasticity) that controls the brain's capacity to control behavior of learning and memory. So, sleeping well is very much associated with the brain's memory improvement.

8.   Reduce Stress and Laugh More

Stress and depression can actually take a toll on one's ability to remember things. However, by engaging yourself in laughter, you reduce the levels of your stress and improve the capabilities of your memory. In a nutshell, laughter brings down the cortisol stress hormone.

Sometimes, we put so much stress on ourselves without even realizing the bad impact that it is having on our health and brain. It puts way more pressure on the heart and when it comes to the brain, you experience a lack in its memory power. Laughter is indeed a great medicine to get rid of this situation! With the help of emotional responses, only a few parts of the brain are activated but, with laughter, all the regions of the brain are engaged. This is the reason, it is helpful to spend time with light-hearted people and laugh everyday as it is one of the proven tricks to boost your memory.

9.   Chew Gum

Chewing gum helps to remember more. People who chew gum test both the short-term and long-term memory. These gum-chewers are deemed to produce higher scores than those who do not chew gum when it comes to remembering things. It is difficult to explain the scientific reasons behind this but, over time, it has shown some effective results for people who are keen to know "how can I improve my memory?"

10. Learn a New Skill

They say keeping your brain busy with learning new things has a good impact on improving your memories. This is also one of the best memory improvement tricks that everyone must apply. The question here is - does age have anything to do with this process. It is seen that keeping your brain busy with purposeful and meaningful activities improves the neurological system and this is how to boost your memory. Science has already proved that this has no relevance with age.

It's always been true that if you want to enhance your brain you must work on it. Learning a new skill that you were initially unfamiliar with has a significant effect on improving your brain. People who always engage their brains in learning new things always demonstrate improved memory function. As a person gets older, by trying new things, he/she ensures a healthy mind.

11. Try Mnemonic Devices

In our everyday life, we come across a lot of things and we can't really keep all of them in our memory. Probably, we don't want to store all of them in the memory. But, what about those incidents, names, events, dates that you want to keep in your memory but face challenges? You can simply try Mnemonic devices as one of the best tricks to boost your memory.

Mnemonic devices are basically memory techniques that aid the brain to encode better, and importantly, remember some fine, but important details. An example of a mnemonic device is the famous '30 days hath September' rhyme which is very significant in helping so many of us to remember how many days in each calendar month. Sometimes, without mnemonic devices, it's often harder to remember some things. Regarding new studies, these techniques highly improve the state of your memory.

There are many other similar devices that you can be applied for this purpose but, the best thing you can do is to innovate some own techniques to improve memory. It works excellent!

12. Association

Every piece of information that we think of is always linked to another piece in one way or another. Our memory basically works by association. For better remembrance, we always try to create an association between pieces of information. When two bits of information are related to each other, we have a greater capability to be creative in linking the two and, as a result this enhances our memories.

13. Rhymes

This may sound like an old-school method, but sometimes, forming rhymes really help memorizing things much better. Our brain is not configured to remember multiple things at the same time but, forming those details in a rhyme structure is helpful to keep them in mind and apply at the right time. This is the best guide to improve memory. After practicing it for a particular time, it becomes very exciting for anyone to remember things in the form of rhymes.

It's always easier to forget a list of six items in a shopping list than it is to forget the lyrics of a song you have not heard for ages. Basically, our brains easily remember things by rhymes since they are linked to each other. Therefore, a person who knows a poem can more easily remember it than remembering random words. This is an excellent way in which you can enhance your brains since you can rhyme things making them exciting and memorable.

14. Flash Cards

Flashcards are commonly used in schools and institutions to help learn school subject material. With flashcards, you are able to remember things like vocabulary and questions about a subject. Flashcards require you to take time so that you can make the studies more useful and memorizing more effective. Through the use of flashcards, you can greatly boost your memory.

15. Organize Your Life

This is an amazing fact to know that the first thing you do after lifting yourself up from the bed to the last thing you do before going to sleep has an impact on our memory. The more organized your life is, the better your memory will become. Your regular activities, food habits and even your sleeping habits - all these have significant impact on the memory.

When your life is organized, it basically means you can distinctly identify one item you are doing from another. An organized life means that the brain works at a certain procedure. This becomes very important when it comes to remembering some things. Therefore, an organized life is a good recipe for an excellent memory capacity.

Moreover, when you do things in an organized way, the brain can also work in an organized manner and that is directly related to the improving of your memory.

CHAPTER 21
TIPS TO HELP YOU
REMEMBER INFORMATION

The human mind has a virtually unlimited memory capacity. The problem for most people is recalling information when it's needed. Memory research and techniques employed by actors, and others who have to memorize a lot, provide some hints that might make it easier.

Suppose we were faced with the task of remembering thousands of spoken lines for an upcoming presentation. Many people would think that involves sitting down in front of a printed script and spending weeks or months to memorize each line. But that's not the most efficient way, and it's not how real actors do it.

In a recent study, trained actors were individually asked to recite their lines from a play that they had previously participated in, but had not looked at in over a year. Most could not recall their lines. But when the actors were put together on a stage and asked to act out scenes from the play, including spoken lines, body movements, and gestures, their recall was almost perfect.

This suggests a couple of things. First, memory makes heavy use of action and movement. A study found that actors were better able to recall lines that were to be spoken while making a physical movement, such as walking across the stage, than lines spoken while standing or sitting still. Second, we remember things better in context than alone. Good actors don't think about their lines, but rather feel their character's thoughts and emotions in response to what the other characters do. This makes remembering their lines more natural and spontaneous. According to the famous actor Michael Caine, "You must be able to stand there not thinking of that line. You take it off the other actor's face."

This way of memorization that involves physical, as well as mental and emotional activities is called active experiencing and has been found to help prevent decline of mental functions in old age. Senior adults who participated in a four-week course in acting showed significantly improved word-recall and problem-solving abilities, compared to similar adults who did not. These improvements persisted for months afterward, and were accompanied by significant improvement in the seniors' perceived quality of life.

What does this mean for you? If you want or need to memorize some information, two effective ways to help you do it are to associate the new information with something already familiar, and to engage a physical activity in the memorization. Suppose your office gets a new software product that you are responsible for learning and using. Make associations with the software it replaced. How are they the same? How are they different? How will the major differences affect your job? When you meet a new person, associate that person's name and appearance with others whom you already know. If you're trying to remember what someone said in a meeting, picture the meeting in your mind. Evoke the feel of the conference table, the faces of the participants, even the smell of the coffee. Recall what else was said in the meeting around that time. Making associations can help you remember by putting information in context.

Engaging a physical activity can also help with memorization. Instead of just reading about how to set up the new software product, actually run through the steps, and then mentally rehearse the sequence of keystrokes and mouse clicks again. Move your arms and fingers as though you are clicking a mouse and typing commands. Engaging your entire body instead of just your mind can help cement the procedure in your memory.

CHAPTER 22
TO IMPROVE YOUR SPEECH, IMPROVE YOUR MEMORY

Life passes us by so quickly, it seems like a blur sometimes. With instant, frenetic input coming from all angles via the internet, television, mobile devices, even electronic billboards, our minds are trained to absorb and purge information at a frightening pace.

But if you want to improve your ability to speak naturally in front of a group, you're going to need to understand how to remember what you want to say and how you want to say it. And if you want to be interesting to listen to, you're going to need to read a lot and you're going to need to remember what you read.

So, very early on in this course, I want to take some time to discuss how to improve your memory. Here are a few suggestions to get you started,based on trying to remember things you read, but you'll need to find what works best for you!

Scan before you read: If you're reading something you're going to want to remember, take a few minutes before you start reading to scan the material. Make note of any subheadings, any sidebars, images or supplementary information. Try to get a feel for the overall thrust of the writer's point or argument. That way, when you start reading, you'll know what to expect and your brain will be able to concentrate more on remembering what you're reading than on interpreting it.

Read with a pencil in hand: Underline main points you want to remember, especially major connecting details that carry the argument from one main point to the next. The more you can highlight that flow of thought, the more readily you'll be able to bring it back to mind when you need to. Just be careful not to underline too much, or you'll defeat the purpose!

Take a moment to reflect: As you read, pause occasionally, such as at headings or chapter breaks, to reflect briefly on what you've learned, how it relates to what you've read previously and what you know is coming up. Let your mind make natural connections between what you're reading and what you already know about the subject being discussed. By taking these brief breaks to reflect and rejuvenate, you're not only sinking important points into your memory, you're also improving your stamina for reading and study!

Try to visualize what you read: If the author is using an illustration to make a point, don't just blow through it. Really try to picture what he's talking about. Make your picture shocking or funny. Make it memorable! Then, when it comes time to recall what you read, that picture that made an impression on you will come back to you!

Review at a later time: If you make the time to review what you've read or studied a half hour, an hour, or a day later, you'll usually find some of it has stuck, but most of it hasn't. You're partway there! Now just go back and look over those points you didn't recall when you reviewed. Then, review again. Your "forgotten" portions should be shrinking each time.

Discuss it with someone else: If it's practical, discuss what you've read with someone else within a day or so. Talking about something helps cement it in your brain.

While these points are specific to remembering things you read, they are just as applicable to remembering what you want to say. While I DO NOT recommend going up in front of a group with a manuscript of your speech in front of you, I also don't recommend writing up a bare bones outline of what you want to say and winging it each time you practice.

Your best bet for improving in your public speaking is to write up what you want to say and practice it repeatedly. Then, make up an outline or note cards with JUST the main points and a few salient connecting details to make the thoughts clear. By using the tips above, you can improve your recall of your original manuscript speech when your pared down outline or notes jogs your memory!

CHAPTER 23
PERSONALITY AND PSYCHOLOGY IN THE WORKPLACE

You probably think of the workplace as the arena for carrying out tasks, earning a living and with luck, experiencing the fulfillment of a job well done. In reality, it's the place where people spend a lot of time playing out complex and often counter-productive dynamics with their colleagues, supervisors and employees.

Understanding how your own and other people's personality and psychology affect your interactions in the workplace can make the difference between a frustrating, unhappy work experience and a successful, fulfilling one. Intelligence and hard work, while necessary ingredients for a positive work-life aren't enough. You'll need to have (or to develop) emotional intelligence.

Emotional intelligence, or the "EQ," is a combination of several psychological functions which are separate from what is measured by IQ tests. Whereas the latter involves comprehension, memory and the ability to analyze and synthesize data, the former pertains to judgment, insight, intuition, impulse control, empathy, reasonableness, personal accountability and integrity.

If you have a high EQ, you are both self-aware and have some understanding and empathy toward other people. You accept yourself while recognizing your own deficiencies, and you see the truth about your choices and behavior without resorting to harsh self-criticism. Your self-knowledge is in service of self- improvement and an optimized work performance.

Emotional intelligence also involves recognizing that other people's behavior is driven by underlying, often unconscious motivations or inner conflicts. This behavior might sometimes appear illogical, but with a high EQ you recognize that it's meaningful, and as a result, you're better equipped to deal with it. With emotional intelligence, you can navigate relationships based on both the overt and subtle needs and intentions of both parties.

People gain emotional intelligence while growing up: loving, nurturing parents are instrumental in its development. Those who were deprived of a fully positive childhood are often deficient in this type of intelligence to a greater or lesser degree, and a lower EQ is demonstrated by ongoing inter-personal difficulties in the workplace. Fortunately, emotional intelligence can be developed later in life through various means, including counseling, coaching, and courses of study.

There are three essential tasks which you'll need to

master at work, and two of them are interpersonal, as opposed to specifically job-related. This makes having a high EQ more important than any other attribute for avoiding problems and achieving success in the workplace. The first and most obvious work task is doing the actual job, but this may be less important than those which follow.

The next essential task is dealing with your boss. They may be someone who is supportive, laissez-faire, inappropriately chummy, overly-critical or even downright abusive. In order to avoid unnecessary stress at work, you should make every attempt to forge an alliance with this person.

You don't even have to like them, (or they, you) but if you are strategic, and demonstrate to your boss that enabling your success is in their best interest, you're likely to obtain their support. You must also recognize & deal with the overly-familiar or critical boss and right from the start, establish good boundaries with them. You are responsible for showing them how you expect to be treated.

If you have a high EQ, you'll understand that most bosses want to know that they didn't make a mistake in hiring you, and that you're an asset, as opposed to a burden. You'll need to look competent yet not set up unreasonable expectations, and demonstrate dedication while not being a martyr to the job. When you make a mistake, you must find a way to demonstrate to the boss that this is an isolated incident, as opposed to an indication of a general lack of competence.

Bringing interpersonal conflicts to your boss's attention might backfire on you, if they perceive you as a complainer, a trouble-maker or someone who is adding to their already considerable work-load. Telling on someone for stealing your idea or your work or for doing something unethical is also fraught with risk, as some of their taint could rub off on you.

You need to ask yourself why you become so irate when people do the wrong thing, and why you feel compelled to police your colleagues. Also, if people are stealing from you in the workplace, perhaps there's a lesson in it for you about more carefully guarding your ideas. Your co-worker's bad behavior and your reactions to it both derive from the inner workings of your psyches.

Some people are prone to throwing themselves on their sword when they make an error; those with a high EQ recognize that it's preferable to find a way to reassure the boss that this error is out of character for you. If you are too quick to point out your faults to your boss, this is a sign of low self-esteem, which needs to be dealt with somewhere other than the work-place.

Some people become frustrated at work when they've performed their tasks competently and responsibly and yet see other, far less capable people being advanced ahead of them. If this has been your experience, perhaps your lack of belief in yourself has been picked up on a subliminal level by your boss, who promoted the individual with a (perhaps undeservedly) stronger sense of self.

Sadly, the narcissistic personality tends to do well in the workplace, as this type is viewed by the boss as confident, competent and deserving of rewards, even when they merely appear to be so. On the other hand, the inadequate personality is doomed to suffer at work. This type does everything required of them but is hyper-critical toward themselves. They will frequently be passed up for promotion as their self-doubt will cause their boss to doubt their abilities, too.

The third essential task at work is dealing with colleagues. You need to appear pleasant yet not come across as a pushover. It's very important to get along with others at work, but trying too hard to please the people you work with will result in their attempting to take advantage of you. In the power-politics of a hierarchical workplace, demonstrating too great a need for approval is read as weakness and garners contempt. Your colleagues are no more the source of emotional nurturing than your boss is.

Coming in late or sitting at your desk unoccupied are

things which will annoy your co-workers and if brought to the attention of your boss could result in your being accused of lowering staff morale. Often, chronic lateness is a way of indirectly expressing resentment. If you have this problem, it would be helpful to address it with a professional.

If you don't have enough to do, or if you tend to finish your work tasks more quickly than your co-workers, you have a few choices: request greater challenges, take on an independent project or find a way to look busy, even when you're not, but remember that each of these choices comes with possible consequences. Those with a high EQ at work know to go about their business in the same way as a defensive driver.

People take their emotional baggage to the workplace. There are those who shirk their responsibilities at work, and those who are overly-conscientious. The former have a sense of entitlement or resentment toward their role, while the latter are looking for parental-type love and approval from their boss for being a "good child."

It's important to understand that the workplace is not the arena for emotional healing, and that the only outcome of sacrificing yourself for your job is burn-out. You must also recognize that there will always be those who'll lie, cheat, steal ideas or materials and avoid work, as a result of their unresolved anger or troubled personalities.

People with a high EQ know that they can either be strategic in dealing with such individuals, or, if there are one or more truly toxic individuals in the workplace, it might be time to look for a new job. Workplace conflicts can create opportunities for you to learn new interpersonal skills or they can be a way in which you recreate an old, counter-productive family dynamic.

Those with a high EQ understand that no job is ever worth tolerating disrespect for. Some people feel a sense of helplessness or desperation at work, not believing in their own ability to be assertive or to find something better. If you are feeling unhappy or resentful at work, you aren't doomed to tolerate the situation, interminably.

Having emotional intelligence enables you to recognize that although you don't necessarily have control, you have a choice about how you deal with each and every work situation. You see that personal empowerment not only enables you to walk away from a dysfunctional work environment; it makes it possible for you to find another, better position.

Taking responsibility for yourself at work can make things much better for you. If you are someone who has gone from job to job, always being bullied or mistreated by co-workers, it might be time to ask yourself if there's something that you're doing which could be provoking this pattern of behavior in others. After all, the common denominator in this equation is you.

If your colleagues, and perhaps even your boss are constantly coming to you with their problems, and you are feeling burdened by your role as the emotional care-taker of your workplace, again, you've created a situation, based on your own emotional issues, which isn't working for you.

CHAPTER 24
THE PSYCHOLOGICAL
DIMENSIONS OF MASOCHISM

The Psychological Dimensions of Masochism. Learning about the world of S&M has been an invaluable experience to me. I had to admit to myself that, viewed from the perspective of what I knew about the nature of the individual self, masochism puzzled me by flying in the face of everything that was rational about the nature of the human personality. People want to be happy and to avoid pain and suffering. They seek to maintain and increase their control over themselves and their surroundings. And they desire to maintain and increase their prestige, respect, and esteem. Viewed from the perspective of these three principles about the self, masochism is a startling paradox. The self is developed to avoid pain, but masochists seek pain. The self strives for control, but masochists seek to relinquish control. The self aims to maximize its esteem, but masochists deliberately seek out humiliation.

Men would talk of the frustration of being unable to entice their wives or partners, who found these sexual activities to be perverse, into engaging in the sexual behaviors that they most longed for.

I suspected that there was a vast number of people who felt tremendous shame and isolation about masochistic submissive longings. I decided to check the clinical literature on masochism to better arm myself with some psychodynamic understanding of why these men, who so often felt shame-bound, were so keen to be dominated, hurt, tortured and humiliated by strong, dominate women.

This is what my research revealed: According to the Diagnostic and Statistical Manual of the American Psychiatric Association, (the shrink's bible), anyone who engages regularly in masochistic sex is mentally ill by definition. There is a long tradition of regarding masochism as the activity of mentally ill sick individuals. Freud described masochism as a perversion. One of his followers linked masochism to cannibalism, criminality, necrophilia and vampirism. Another analyst said that all neurotics are masochistics. In short, clinical perspectives have regarded masochists as seriously disturbed.

Krafft-Ebing, the nineteenth-century psychiatrist who coined the term, subsumed masochism under the broad heading of "General Pathology" in this famous volume, Psychopath Sexualize, in 1876. Masochism became a pathological, sexual and psychopathic phenomenon all at once.

"By masochism I understand a particular perversion of the psychical sexual life in which the individual affected, in sexual feeling and thought, is controlled by the idea of being completely and unconditionally subject to the will of a person of the opposite sex; of being treated by this person as a master -- humiliated and abused. This idea is colored by lustful feeling; the masochist lives in fantasies, in which he creates situations of this kind and often attempts to realize them. By this perversion his sexual instinct is often made more or less insensible to the normal charms of the opposite sex - incapable of a normal sexual life - psychically impotent."

It has become practically a dogma of psychoanalytic thought that masochism is a sexual condition in which punishment is required before satisfaction can be reached. Freud understood the phenomenon as resulting from an "unconscious feeling of guilt" as "a need for punishment by some parental authority. Writing in 1919, Freud found the genesis and reference point for masochism in the Oedipus-complex. Masochism, he said, actually begins in infantile sexuality, when the wish for the incestuous connection with mother or father must be repressed. Guilt enters at this point, in connection with incestuous wishes. The parent figure then becomes the dispenser of punishment instead of love and appears in desires for beating, spanking, etc. The fantasy of being beaten becomes the meeting place between the sense of guilt and sexual love. Whether it involves literal pain or not, the punishment desired by the masochist is enjoyed in and of itself. Punishment and satisfaction both give pleasure - and humiliation. Freud, in referring to masochism as a "perversion", cemented it forever in the ghetto of the aberrant and deviant.

My research, however, did not jibe with my clinical reality. The people who presented to me were not immature or inferior. In fact, the reverse seemed to be the case. Masochists are more likely to be successful by social standards: professionally, sexually, emotionally, culturally, in marriages or out. They are frequently individuals of inner strength of character, possessed of strong coping skills with an ethical sense of individual responsibility. A famous study of the "sexual profile of men in power" found to the researchers' surprise, a high quantity of masochistic sexual activity among successful politicians, judges and other important and influential men.

It became obvious to me that psychology's theories of masochism were obsolete. In the 1960's, homosexuality was deleted from the DSMIV and was recognized not as a pathology, but as a lifestyle choice. It is my contention that the same should be done with masochism and that, like homosexuality, it needs to be removed from the rubric of "psychopathology" and be seen for what it is: a sexual lifestyle choice. It is the intention of this paper to suggest ways of understanding masochism without invoking theories of mental illness.

The questions, however, remained. I puzzled as to why so many men, raised in a culture that valued masculine initiative, assertiveness, and dominance, want to be relieved of these qualities and surrender their will to a strong, dominant woman who might torture, control and humiliate them. What was the basis of this compelling urge to surrender and serve, to relinquish control, to accept physical pain and emotional humiliation?

Ritualized suffering seemed to be a way of giving meaning and value to human infirmities. After all, there is no paucity of suffering in human life. None of us need go looking for pain. The suffering of helplessness, disappointment, loss, powerlessness and limitation, is a part of the human condition. It is my hunch that there is something like a universal need, wish or longing for surrender completely to certain aspects of human life and that it assumes many forms. This passionate longing to surrender comes into play in at least some instances of masochism. Submission, losing oneself to the power of the other, becoming enslaved to the master is the ever-available lookalike to surrender.

Submissives speak of a quality of liberation, freedom and expansion of the self in a scene as a situation similar to the letting down of defensive barriers. They speak of the experience of complete vulnerability. I believe that buried or frozen, is a longing for something in the environment to make possible surrender, a sense of yielding of the false self. The false self is an idea developed by a famous psychoanalyst who posited that most parents need their children to behave in circumscribed ways in order for the child to receive their love. For a child, parental love is a matter of survival, and so the child forges a "self" that they think will ensure parental love and approval. The false self is usually a "caretaker" self. A Scene sometimes allows for years of defensive barriers that support the false self to be broken through. It carries with it a longing for the birth of the true self. Deep down we long to give up, to "come clean", as part of a general longing to be known or recognized. The prospect of surrender may be accompanied by a feeling of dread and or relief or even ecstasy. It is an experience of being "in the moment", totally in the present. Its ultimate direction is the discovery of one's identity, one's sense of self, of one's sense of wholeness, even one's sense of unity with other living beings. Joyous in spirit, it transcends the pain that evokes it. One's exquisite pain is sometimes akin to mystical ecstasy. Within the context of that surrender, a self-negating submissive experience occurs in which the person is enthralled by the dominant partner. The intensity of the masochism is a living testimonial of the urgency with which some buried part of the personality is screaming to be released. The surrender is nothing less than a controlled dissolution of self-boundaries.

The deeper yearning is the longing to be reached,

known and accepted in a safe environment which narcissistic, dysfunctional or preoccupied parents were unable to provide the child at a young age.

Fantasies of being raped, which are very common, can have all manners of meanings. Among them, one will almost always find, sometimes deeply buried, a yearning for deep surrender. The submissive longs for and wishes to be found, recognized, penetrated to the core, so as to become real, or, as one analyst says it "to come into being."

In addition to the longing to surrender into a truer sense of self, masochistic behaviors have another meaning. People need and take delight in fantasy production. Ask the Disneyland folk who cater to adults as much as to children. Scenes have tremendous potential for potentiating fantasy. Costumes, rituals, scenarios, an endless variety of sex props, and elaborate sets reveal of the richness the creative inner life and speak to the very real human need for fantasy play. The fantasies are the carriers of a full spectrum of human feelings: to control, to be controlled, to tease, to be teased, to play, to please, and to achieve solace from the confines of the mundaness of ordinary life. They represent the suspension of normal reality that is an occasional necessity for all healthy people.

Probably the last thing masochism appears aimed at is

balance. In keeping with its paradoxical nature, masochism provides not so much a state of weakness, but a sense of surrender, receptivity and sensitivity. Masochism is the condition of submitting fully to an experience, which counters lives that, in our Western society, are ego-centered, constrained, rational, and competitive. Strength can be a terrible burden. It is a constraint, which can be relieved in moments of abandonment, of letting down and letting go. So it is hardly surprising that the pull of masochistic experiences should be so strong in a culture the overvalues ego strength at the expense of a fuller experience of all dimensions of psychic life.

CHAPTER 25
WAYS TO MAKE FRIENDS
WITH YOUR NEW NEIGHBORS

You are more than excited because you feel like you are also moving forward to a new, bright life. You started your day by decorating your new home with your equally new furniture and home accessories. In fact, you have spent two and a half days to complete everything. What is more important to you, though, is that you and your family are finally settled. But, you are forgetting something - what about the neighborhood? Coming along with your new home is a new community, where you are currently a total stranger. As a new arrival, it is a best gesture if you will be the one to approach them, introduce yourself and offer friendship. However, if you have no idea what are the best ways to do this, consider this list:

Invite them to your housewarming party.

Being in your new home gives you the opportunity to host a housewarming party. Instead of inviting just your friends and relatives, invite also your new neighbors. In this way, you are already extending your family to them.

Offer them your food.

Grill barbecue in your front yard. Set a table for you

and your family. But, make sure you have aplenty of barbecue, so when you see neighbors around, you will be able to offer each of them with a stick of barbeque. Just a stick, but it will mark a new beginning of friendship.

Propose a handshake to people you meet along the neighborhood.

When you are walking along the area, offer a handshake to people outside of their homes. Introduce yourself and your family. This gesture will enable them to understand that you are opening your doors to them.

Attend community events.

If you receive invitation for a community event, do not have a second thought in attending. Grace the occasion. In this way, you will be introduced to majority of your neighbors. You can easily make friends with them.

Join community organizations.

Involve yourself in community organizations. By becoming a member of one or two organizations, you will engage in activities that will require your regular attendance; hence, it will be too soon that you will gain friends.

Offer your help to those who are in need.

In time of emergencies, your neighbors, aside from

your house members, are the closest to you. If you feel like they need your help, offer them one. For instance, if one of them requires assistance in gardening, offer your help.

Take a walk.

Each morning, try to take a walk, along with your family, if possible. By seeing you every day, they will take notice of you and they will offer a smile. It will become the start of a new life in the neighborhood.

By following one if not all of these tips, you will realize, meeting and making friends with your new neighbors is not a difficult task to do. In fact, it is an enjoyable and a funny thing to look back on after you have already tied your friendship with them.

CHAPTER 26
RELEVANT EDUCATION FOR A KNOWLEDGE-BASED ECONOMY

Education is a human right issue for both personal enrichment and development. This is also supported by goal 4 for Sustainable Development Goals of the 2030 Agenda for Sustainable Development. Goal 4 aim to ensure inclusive and equitable quality education and promote lifelong learning opportunities for all. Today's world is ever changing rapidly, in terms of social, economic, political and digital connectivity and usage. The changes requires individuals to adapt and adopt by acquiring relevant new knowledge, skills, attitudes and competencies in a wide range of settings to remain relevant and unlimited. Lifelong learning opportunities would enable the acquisition of such relevant new knowledge, skills, attitudes and competencies, for individuals to meet life's challenges, remain relevant and sustain their lives, communities and societies in this digital world.

According to Toffler (1970) "the illiterates of the 21st century will not be those who cannot read and write, but those who cannot learn, unlearn and relearn". Lifelong learning is about learning, unlearning and relearning through acquiring and updating all kinds of abilities, interests, knowledge and qualifications from the pre-school years to post retirement.

Learning means the acquisition of knowledge or skills through study, experience, or being taught. Unlearning is seen as deleting and replacing obsolete knowledge. Relearning means learn material that has been previously learned and then forgotten. Lifelong learning activities promote the development of knowledge and competencies that will enable adaptations to knowledge-based societies, while at the same time valuing all forms of learning. Lifelong learning (LL) is therefore an indispensable guiding principle of educational development.

The commonly understood definition of lifelong learning is 'all learning undertaken throughout life which is ongoing, voluntary and self-motivated in the pursuit of knowledge, skills, attitudes and competencies for either personal or professional reasons.

What is Lifelong Learning?

The provision of learning through formal, informal and non-formal learning opportunities throughout people's lives with the purpose of fostering continuous development and improvement of knowledge and skills needed for employment, community service and/or

personal fulfilment. As could be deduced from this definition, lifelong learning is all-encompassing and integral
to the vision of a knowledge-based economy and/or
society. Lifelong learning can enhance our understanding
of the world around us, provide us with more and better
opportunities and improve our quality of life.

Types/categories of lifelong learning learners

- Skill-seeking - Learners who need to attain
  new or improved skills for the purpose of
  bettering themselves and be able to solve the
  challenges they face (or meet in the future) in
  their lives.

- Problem-centred - Learners who only want to
  learn specific skills needed to deal with a
  specific problem that they have encountered or
  might encounter in their particular life situations.

- Task-centred - Learners who only want to concentrate on tasks directed towards reaching
  some specific goals or solving a specific
  problem.

- Life-centred - Learners with great experience
  background and faced with a variety of issues
  in their everyday life and want to focus their

attention on real-world/life challenges/situations and solving real-world problems. They also want to focus on applying newly gained knowledge and/or skills to everyday and real-world situations.

- Solution-driven - Learners who are interested in focusing their efforts to solving problems in real life situations, especially those found in their immediate communities and/or environments or dealing with tasks directed towards reaching specific goals or solutions.

- Value-driven - learners who require guidance why they should participate in learning endeavours and what benefit is there for them. These learners need to be motivated by other to explain to them why they should learn.

- Externally motivated - Learners who are motivated by such factors as better jobs, better salaries, and increased promotional opportunities.

- Internally motivated - Learners who possess strong internal motivation to learn, such as developing their self-esteem, confidence, recognition, career satisfaction, gaining skills to manage their time better or improving the overall quality of life for their families or communities or both.

- Active learners - Learners who are just willing to participate in the learning process (they could be internally or externally motivated or no motivation at all).

- Hands-on - Learners who prefer learning by doing rather than by listening and interested in being provided with opportunities to apply their newly gained skills right away.

- Self-directed - Learners who perceive themselves to be independent and responsible for their own learning, planning and directing their own learning activities. According to Fisher, King and Tague (2001) a self-directed learner takes control and accepts the freedom to learn what they view as important for them.

- Expert /experienced-based - Learners are practicing (working) in a specific field and want to gain knowledge/skills in that specific field for the purpose of improving their practice. These learners bring real-life experiences to the learning situations, thereby influencing the learning process and make it relevant.

- Independent - Learners who are more self-reliant and learn by utilising previously gained knowledge, skills and work experience in order to accomplish things for themselves. These learners rely on their own personal experiences, strengths and knowledge in seeking answers to problems and to solving such problems

Why do we need lifelong learning?

- Upgrade job

- Start a business

- Learn about a subject or to extend their knowledge

- Meet new people

- Develop self-confidence

- Participate in social networking

- Develop personal skills

- Individual's capacity for lifelong learning

- Capacity to set personal objectives in a realistic manner

- Effectiveness in applying knowledge already possessed

- Efficiency in evaluating one's own learning

- Skills to locate the required information

- Effectiveness in using different learning strategies and learning in different settings

- Skills to use learning aids and resources, such as libraries, media and/or the internet

- Ability to use and interpret materials from different subject areas

The benefits of lifelong learning to society

- From those critical statements regarding the importance of lifelong learning it emerges that lifelong learning holds both private and public benefits. The benefits of lifelong learning to society, business and the individual include, among others:

- The economic benefits of lifelong learning both for employment purposes and high earnings are regarded by many as the most important. People who have no jobs engage in lifelong learning in order to gain employable skills and to make a living. Those with jobs engage in lifelong learning so that they can upgrade their skills to be able to be promoted to higher positions in their jobs and earn more money.

- Enhanced employability which means lifelong learning adds value to the person's ability to gain productive employment and make greater economic contribution to his/her organisation and to society as a whole. This is because lifelong learning enables more people to gain skills and competencies required for the job market.

- Reduced expenditure in unemployment and other social benefits and early retirement (in countries that have those benefits), which means if there are more people with skills and being productive government will concentrate the limited resources to developing infrastructure and create jobs rather than spending it on people who are unable to find work or not willing to work. Infrastructure development means more good educational and health facilities as well as roads and other transport infrastructure for promoting economic development. More jobs means there are more people contributing to government income through taxes and supporting the overall development of the country.

- Reduced criminal activities in societies that have high unemployment rates (Namibia is a good example) of which many of the criminal activities are due to citizens who have nothing productive to do, but having a lot of time on their hands to be idling and/or engaging in mischievous and unproductive activities. Lifelong learning opportunities enable people to gain useful skills and competencies so that they are more employable and there are plenty of opportunities for people to be engaged in productive and worthy causes. We are told that criminal activities are on the increase in societies where there is high unemployment, high illiteracy and /or less educated citizenry as well as where there are high levels of poverty.

- Increased high social returns in terms of civic participation and community involvement in activities that are aimed at improving the standards of living of all people in society. Lifelong learning enables citizens to be active in community development activities and thereby improving their health and well-being as well as generating and nurturing creative ideas for business and innovation development. Lifelong learning also increases high social returns in terms of civic participation and community involvement, for instance volunteering for good causes in their communities and societies thereby enabling government to save through increased civil society involvement.

;Career development in the age of lifelong learning

Lifelong learning has been more linked to improving work activities through improving workers' attitudes towards work and their productive capacities. Workplace learning whether formal, non-formal or informal is targeted to career development of employees. Lifelong learning helps people to develop their potential and the knowledge, skills, attitudes and competencies required for the job market. They are required to constantly learn at the workplace. For the lifelong learning system to work at the workplace, where learning is mainly informal, there must be a self-regulating system that enable employees to access relevant information about the labour market and development in the economy. It has been proven across the world that people who are educated are more likely to find decent employment than those with no education. This mean that lifelong learning is currently being used for career development and progress in the labour market as much as it is being used for leisure and community development purposes.

Career development is an important aspect for the labour market as all employees aim for higher salaries, promotions and other incentives that comes with one's job or employment contract.

Eraut (2007) found that most of the workplace learning of mid-career professionals is largely done in an informal way through consultation and collaboration. The joy of learning and the opportunity to apply the newly acquired skills to the workplace are the best sources of motivation for learning in one's life.

Approaches to learning at the workplace

Eraut (2004) have identified five approaches for the knowledge, skills, attitudes and competencies for lifelong learning at the workplace.

• Group learning: participation in group activities such as team-working towards a common goal or outcome or group set up to work on special projects or for a special purpose. These circumstances will force members of the group to learn communally in order to accomplish their tasks.

- On the job training through social learning activities allows employees to observe others and learn as they learn new practices, new perspectives as they work alongside each other on a routine task or specific project.

- On the job training through understudy / deputizing allow employees to learn from those with more expertise than them but working in the same organisation / institution.

- On the job training by external expertise (consultants) through performance audits, consultancies, workshops.

- Assessment activities such as monitoring and evaluation are some of the approaches used by organisations to enable employees learn about their progress and address gaps.

Work processes through which employees learn better

- Group participation process: through asking questions and participating in decisions;

- Tackling challenging assignments/tasks/ roles;

- Through being supervised, coached and being mentored, shadowing and or reflecting;

- Working alongside colleagues, locating resource persons within the organisation as well as listening and observing others;

- Through problem solving, trying things out, suing models or mediating artefacts and learning through mistakes;

- Consultation with other employees and management;

- Visiting other sites/attending conferences and

participating in short courses;

- Working with clients;

- Consolidating/ extending/ giving and receiving feedback;

- Working/studying for a qualification, working for a reward.

Factors affecting modes of learning in the workplace

Learning factors

The factors that enable employees to be proactive in seeking learning opportunities

- Challenging and value of the work: under challenged and over challenged might impact negatively on the person's ability to learn;

- Feedback and support;

- Confidence and commitment; and

- The ability to recognise learning opportunities

Work context factors

The factors that attract the employees to the organisation and motivate them to learn and contribute to the goals of the organisation.

- Feedback and support (especially during the few months in a new job);

- Allocation and structuring of work;

- Encounters and relationship with people at wok; and

- Expectations of each person's role, performance and progress.

Suggestions for employers

Promote Media and Information Literacy (MIL) to enables employees to be informed readers in today's hyper connected world.

MIL enables employees to interpret the complex messages they receive in today's hyper connected world.

CONCLUSION

Understanding body language along with verbal cues can be useful in communicating and understanding others. It can be fun, but you're not a psychic, you can't read minds or interpret what someone is thinking or feeling. Use these techniques to find clues to help you understand other people and communicate better

Success at work is never a matter of merely being competent. Those who rise through the ranks are either clever manipulators who know how to get others to promote them, or excellent negotiators who are able to navigate the minefield of workplace personality and psychology with finesse.

I believe that therapists need to radically alter their approach to doing psychotherapy with masochistic patients. My colleagues complain that masochists are difficult to "cure". Perhaps because the paradigm from which these therapists operate are faulty. The recognition of value and meaning in the desire to suffer humiliation runs counter to the prevailing attitude in psychology. The main thrust of modern theory and practice has been toward ego psychology. The values of psychotherapy have been aimed, for the most part, at building strong, coping, rational problem-solving egos. Ego-values are certainly worthy ones, yet it costs something to gain strength, to cope, to be rational and to solve problems. This may account for the dissatisfaction many people feel after years of psychotherapy. Building a strong ego is only one side of the story; it neglects other, crucial parts of the human psyche. Modern psychology has been in large measure dominated by helping people develop independence, strength, achievement decisive action, coping and planning. What's missing is attention to the more subtle dimensions of soul.

REFERENCES

Eraut, M. (2007). Learning from other people in the workplace. Oxford Review of Education, 33 (4), pp.403-422.

Eraut, M. (2004). Informal learning in the workplace. Studies in Continuing Education, 26, pp. 247-273.

Fisher, M, King, J., &Tague, G. (2001). Development of a self-directed learning readiness scale for nursing education. Nurse Education Today, 21, pp. 516 -525.

The great vision 2000 Odufuwa Seyi

Conventional wisdome report

national institute of health nov 13 2002

Report on national institute of aging

The degree of cognitive decline Dr. Karlene Ball of the University of Alabama at Birmingham

NIA study report

Quoted study on London cab drivers (Proceedings of the National Academy of Science, April 11, 2000 issue)

NBC Philadelphia report On Jun 2, 2005

Experimental reports of Karl Lashley 1920-1929

Report on the study by Larry Feig at Tufts University

School of Medicine in Boston

Benefits of regular aerobic exercise for executive functioning in healthy populations US National Library of Medicine (National Institutes of Health) in February 2013

Cardiovascular fitness, cortical plasticity, and aging; March 2004 National Academy of Sciences

A single bout of resistance exercise can enhance episodic memory performance: November 2014, Acta Psychologica

Toffler, A. (1970). Future shock. New York: Random House.

The books of the admonition of Mother Teresa

Research report of Dr. Albert Mehrabian

World Economic Report

Clinical literature

Do not go yet; One last thing to do

If you enjoyed this book or found it useful I'd be very grateful if you'd post a short review on it. Your support really does make a difference and I read all the reviews personally so I can get your feedback and make this book even better.

Thanks again for your support!